ILLUMINATING STAINED GLASS

ILLUMINATING STAINED GLASS

Creativity, Conservation and Craft at Barley Studio

Juliette MacDonald,
Helen Whittaker & Keith Barley

LUND
HUMPHRIES

First published in 2025 by Lund Humphries

Lund Humphries
Second Home Spitalfields
68-80 Hanbury Street
London
E1 5JL
UK

www.lundhumphries.com

Illuminating Stained Glass: Creativity, Conservation and Craft at Barley Studio © Juliette MacDonald, Helen Whittaker and Keith Barley, 2025
All rights reserved

ISBN: 978-1-84822-672-2

A Cataloguing-in-Publication record for this book is available from the British Library.

Cover and frontispiece: The *Hope* window, 2024, stained glass, 140 × 400 cm, St Michael's Church, Highgate, London
Photograph: Barley Studio Ltd

Copy edited by Pamela Bertram
Designed by Jacqui Cornish
Proofread by Patrick Cole
Cover design by Paul Arnot
Set in Arnhem Pro, Niveau Grotesk and Quasimoda
Printed in Bosnia and Herzegovina

This book is printed on sustainably sourced FSC paper

FSC
www.fsc.org
MIX
Paper | Supporting responsible forestry
FSC® C118234

PICTURE CREDITS

All photographs are courtesy of Barley Studio Ltd, with the exception of the figures listed below which are courtesy of the following copyright holders:

1.2 The British Library Board (Add MS 35211 P ff.46); **2.1a, 2.1b** The late Revd Gordon Plumb © Corpus Vitrearum (Great Britain); **3.3b** Rob Scott Photography; **3.5b** The Royal Air Force Club; **3.6a** Barry Hale; **3.6d** Julian Sullivan; **3.9c** David Harrison; **4.4c** The Royal Air Force Club; **4.5a** Hockney Pictures; **4.6a** David Harrison; **5.2a, 5.2c** Our Lady of Lourdes Catholic Chapel, Filinvest City, Muntinlupa City, Philippines

CONTENTS

Foreword by Loyd Grossman CBE, FSA   6

Introduction   7

1   Conservation and Restoration   9

2   Creativity and Craft   19

3   Concept to Creation   37

4   Change and Continuity   57

5   Contemporary Contexts   73

Conclusion   90

Notes   91
Bibliography   93
Index   94
Acknowledgements   96

FOREWORD

Few are immune to the beauty of light and colour that stained glass provides. Because the craft of making stained glass is so intricate and demanding, many people forget that stained glass is a great art. I can't think of anyone better than Juliette MacDonald, Helen Whittaker, Keith Barley and their colleagues at Barley Studio to explain all the intricacies and inspire us with all the possibilities of this art *and* its craft.

I was surprised and thrilled when I was invited to be an Honorary Liveryman of the Worshipful Company of Glaziers and Painters in Glass – known as the Glaziers for convenience – one of the ancient livery companies of the City of London which has been in business since the 1360s. Through its charitable and educational activities the Glaziers support and celebrate both the history and future of stained glass, and thanks to them I was able to meet many of the practitioners and scholars in the field and also to appreciate the global spread and appeal of the art which flourished from Chicago to Mumbai.

Throughout my work in the heritage sector – a lifelong interest which was formalised with my appointment as a Commissioner for English Heritage in the 1990s – I came to keenly appreciate that the role of stained glass extends far beyond parish churches and cathedrals, and is also very much a living and evolving art form. I was lucky enough to meet Keith in 1998 when I presented him with the Jerwood Award for his conservation work at St Mary's Church, Fairford, Gloucestershire. Some years later, he graciously invited me to speak at a grand dinner during his time as Master of the Glaziers' Company. I got to know Helen when she was head of the Judging Panel for the Stevens Competition and I had the delightful and not very burdensome job of handing out the prizes. Juliette, Helen and Keith share profound knowledge, refined appreciation and immense enthusiasm for all aspects of stained glass which they have masterfully conveyed in this splendid book.

Loyd Grossman CBE, FSA

INTRODUCTION

Throughout the centuries, stained glass has had a capacity to adapt to the ever-evolving cultural, artistic and technological landscapes, enabling the medium to inspire viewers through its unique ability to harness the power of light and colour to uplift our senses.

In 2023, 'stained-glass window making' was added to the Heritage Craft Association's Red List of endangered crafts. This list was first published in 2017 and defines a heritage craft as 'a practice which employs manual dexterity and skill and an understanding of traditional materials, design and techniques, and which has been practised for two or more successive generations'.[1] The list is created to draw attention to the implications of the loss of these skills and to act as a catalyst for people to work together to find ways of ensuring that craft skills continue to flourish in order to enrich our culture. The authors hope that Barley Studio's passion for and commitment to this much-loved art and craft, as demonstrated in this book, will contribute to its appreciation and survival.

Throughout its long heritage, technical developments have always occurred in the production of glass itself and the way it is then treated by a designer and glazier. In the 20th century, the artist John Piper reflected on the balance between tradition and change which could be seen in stained-glass designs. In his book, *Stained Glass: art or anti-art*, written in 1968, Piper observed that when he first began to look at stained glass, he thought it all looked alike. His interest began with identifying and dating windows, but he says that: '[. . .] I became a looker rather than a cataloguer, and now that I have eyes for nothing but its particular impact I am struck by the great *differences* in early glass – not the similarities [. . .].'[2]

Through Piper's careful review of medieval glass, it becomes clear that whilst the basic method of creation adheres to a handmade 'tradition', it is not an unchanging phenomenon.

The conservation of historic windows and creation of contemporary work at Barley Studio over the last 50 years provides an ideal platform to examine and explore the role of stained glass today, with insights from the authors' personal experience as designers, conservators and educators.

Chapter 1, 'Conservation and Restoration', describes Barley Studio's reconstruction and conservation work, particularly focusing on the unique schemes of medieval windows at St Nicholas' Church, Stanford on Avon, Northamptonshire and St Mary's Church, Fairford, Gloucestershire. Keith Barley's observations provide insights on the complexities of conserving glass and highlight the value of challenging the accepted 'rules' inherited from the 19th century. Chapter 2, 'Creativity and Craft', considers Helen Whittaker's work as a practitioner and demonstrates the variety of techniques she uses to engage a contemporary audience. Chapter 3, 'Concept to Creation', considers the key design factors that stimulate Helen's creative approach to each commission. Chapter 4, 'Change and Continuity', reflects on the connections between traditional and contemporary approaches to stained glass. In the final chapter, 'Contemporary Contexts', the authors demonstrate how stained-glass windows can adapt to different settings and survive changes in popular tastes and trends. The range of perspectives presented within this book aim to draw attention to and celebrate the power of this unique art form.

left

1.1a   St Peter, detail of east window, photographed before restoration, July 1984, stained glass, 21.5 × 48.5 cm, St Nicholas' Church, Warndon

right

1.1b   St Peter, detail of east window, photographed after restoration, December 1984, stained glass, 21.5 × 48.5 cm, St Nicholas' Church, Warndon

1

CONSERVATION AND RESTORATION

Keith Barley MBE is the Founder, Managing Director and Head Conservator at Barley Studio and is internationally renowned for his work in stained-glass conservation. He is conservation adviser to the UK Corpus Vitrearum (CVMA), Master Glazier for Ely Cathedral and has consulted for the Metropolitan Museum of Art, New York, the Museum of Fine Art, Boston, St Patrick's Cathedral, New York, and Siena Cathedral. For Keith, conserving and restoring glass is more than just preserving the past, it is also about finding ways to ensure that the stories told through ancient glass are once again legible. He has sought to develop methods of conservation which provide a safe framework for conserved and restored windows and also a stable environment to protect them from the wear and tear of rain and humidity, so that they can survive for many more years.

Keith was the first apprentice of the York Glaziers Trust, formed from York Minster's glazing workshop in 1967. At its inception Dr Peter Newton[1] was appointed as academic advisor to the Trust. Keith recalls that: 'Peter's encyclopaedic knowledge of art history and the lives of the saints filled me with enthusiasm and awe. We were working on the Minster's nave clerestory narrative panels and Peter could decipher a subject from what appeared to me to be a mass of misplaced, corroded and heavily leaded glass. To make these neglected works of art more legible became my desire.'

ST NICHOLAS' CHURCH, WARNDON, WORCESTER

In 1973, Keith set up as an independent stained-glass craftsman and conservator. An early project in collaboration with Peter Newton was for St Nicholas' Church, Warndon in Worcester. 'A forlorn figure of St Peter set against diamond quarries was rearranged to a comprehensible pose and set within a canopy niche typical of the fourteenth century' (figs 1.1a and 1.1b).[2]

ST NICHOLAS' CHURCH, STANFORD ON AVON, NORTHAMPTONSHIRE

In 1984, Keith was selected to conserve the important collection of 14th, 15th and 16th-century stained glass in the 13 windows of St Nicholas' Church, Stanford on Avon, Northamptonshire. The significance of this scheme had been recognised by the 19th-century lawyer and antiquarian Charles Winston, who had visited Stanford on Avon over 100 years previously. Winston's observations of Stanford's windows conclude with a clear account of attitudes to restoration at the time:

> It is impossible to refrain from expressing a hope that the painted glass in Stanford church [. . .] may long remain a splendid monument of ancient art, and an instructive study for the amateur and artist. [. . .] the glass-wright, when he comes, too often obliterates all traces of the original design by arbitrary re-arrangements, made partly with a view to produce a sightly object, partly to save the time required for a more careful investigation. On the whole it seems the safer, and more prudent [. . .], to content ourselves with preserving these venerable relics by timely patching and mending, and transmitting them to posterity as they have

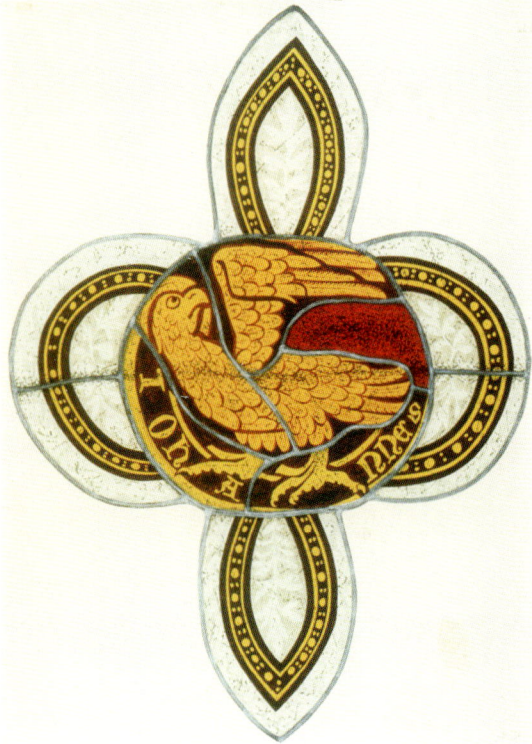

1.2 Charles Winston, Eagle of St John, 1849, drawing on paper, 38.2 × 50 cm, St Nicholas' Church, Stanford on Avon

descended to ourselves, the genuine evidence of ancient art, ungarbled and untampered with.[3]

Keith notes that 'at this point I was unaware of hostility towards restoration following the interventions of the 19th century but I was soon to receive a clear message highlighting this approach to conservation.' He received a letter from the Council for the Care of Churches (CCC) [now the Church Buildings Council] in which they stated:

The Chairman has asked me to stress that approval is given on the strict understanding that there must be no re-arrangement whatsoever without specific approval of the committee.

The only re-arrangement so far agreed is the re-unification of parts of the eagle of St. John [. . .][4]

It is interesting to note that the CCC's concerns are remarkably similar to those expressed by Charles Winston. While acknowledging these concerns, Keith remained committed to his beliefs that by collaboration, research and informed judgement a more comprehensible restoration could be achieved.

The eagle of St John mentioned by the CCC refers to a tracery panel in the north nave aisle which had been drawn by Winston in 1849 (fig.1.2).

1.3 Detail of bishop figure photographed before conservation, July 1991, stained glass, 40 × 86 cm, east window, north nave aisle, St Nicholas' Church, Stanford on Avon

left

1.4a   Tracery light, photographed before conservation, July 1991, stained glass, 39 × 54 cm, north nave aisle, St Nicholas' Church, Stanford on Avon

right

1.4b   Tracery light, photographed after conservation, June 1997, stained glass, 39 × 54 cm, north nave aisle, St Nicholas' Church, Stanford on Avon

Unfortunately, in the intervening years, parts of the glass from the eagle had been removed to use as 'stop-gaps' in the drapery of the figure of a bishop in an entirely different window, using odd fragments of glass to fill the space left behind in the tracery window – exactly the type of 'arbitrary re-arrangement' Winston had warned against. Keith retrieved the original pieces and replaced them in the tracery window (figs 1.3, 1.4a and 1.4b).

Following the successful conservation of the eagle panel, Keith made further proposals for rearrangement of the glass at St Nicholas' Church. He worked initially with the guidance of Peter Newton and, following his death in 1987, with Richard Marks, one of several art historians taught by Peter. In collaboration with Richard, Keith proposed not only to return misplaced pieces to their original locations within panels, but also whole panels to their original window openings. 'Once we had brought all of the windows into the studio, we embarked on the world's biggest jigsaw puzzle! Re-creating the original artists' scheme was a huge endeavour, combining Richard's academic knowledge of iconography with my practical skills, matching the shapes of the glass pieces and panels to their original openings.' Through careful research and communication during meetings at Barley Studio, members of the parish and representatives from English Heritage (acting on behalf of the funders, the National Heritage Memorial Fund) were convinced of the merits of restoration, and finally gave permission for all of the proposed rearrangements.

Having painstakingly conserved and restored the glass of St Nicholas' Church, Keith was also keen that it should be protected from further damage from its environment, in particular the effects of rain and humidity. He had been aware of the possibility of environmental protection since his time at York Minster, and indeed had installed protective glazing to the 15th-century windows of St Michael and All Angels' Church, Ashton under Lyne, as early as 1975. In 1986 he was awarded a Winston Churchill Travelling Fellowship to study mainland European environmental protective glazing systems (then known as 'isothermal glazing') for stained glass. 'My aim was to look at the methods, materials and installation techniques being used and from the study develop a system applicable to typical British glazing situations.' The Stanford on Avon scheme was one of the first to be set within Barley Studio's newly developed environmental protective glazing system.

According to the international Corpus Vitrearum: 'The installation of a protective glazing system is a crucial part of the preventive conservation of architectural stained glass.'[5] Over 50 years of international research and monitoring has demonstrated the efficacy of environmental protective glazing time and again, with the best environmental conditions for the historic glass achieved through internal ventilation of the interspace.

Keith has continued to develop the materials and methods used for protective glazing systems, adopting the principles of simple and cost-effective design, durable materials that are compatible with the related building fabric, and skills and techniques that are compatible with the glazier's craft. He has always sought to share knowledge with other studios and workshops, with the result that similar systems are now used by leading cathedral glass conservation studios such as Canterbury, York and Lincoln, as well as many independent studios throughout the country.

ST MARY'S CHURCH, FAIRFORD, GLOUCESTERSHIRE

Keith's conservation and restoration of the world-famous, late-medieval glazing scheme of St Mary's Church, Fairford, Gloucestershire occupied over two decades of his career. In their artistic quality and technical virtuosity, the Fairford windows are regarded as one of the most important glazing schemes in Europe. The 28 windows were conceived and executed in a single campaign between 1500 and 1515, and remarkably had survived the destruction of the Reformation, the English Civil War and the neglect of subsequent centuries almost intact.

On the accession of Edward VI in 1547, royal injunctions against images in churches were issued. 'They shall take away and destroy all shrines, pictures, paintings and all other monuments of feigned miracles so that there remains no memory of the same in wall, window glass, or elsewhere in our churches or houses.'[6]

At Fairford, protection of the windows by the parish, as well as later restoration, meant that the only evidence of such targeted destruction was the head of Christ and those of the two thieves in the east window, which were completely destroyed, and the head of the transfigured Christ in the east window of the south nave which had been abraded away (fig.1.5a).[7]

Probably the greatest destruction of the windows occurred during the great storm of 1703

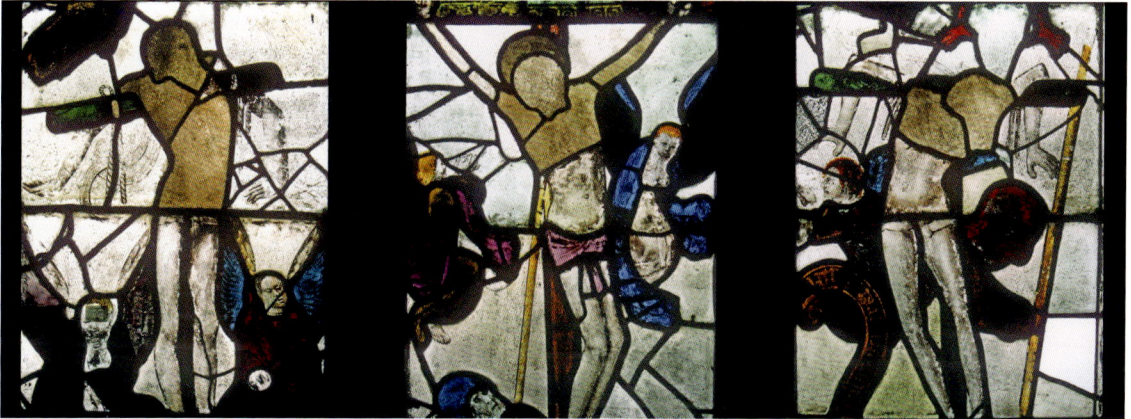

1.5a   Details of east window, 1500–1515, photographed before conservation, December 1990, stained glass, 260 × 490 cm (full window), St Mary's Church, Fairford

1.5b   Details of east window, 1500–1515, photographed after conservation, June 1992, stained glass, 260 × 490 cm (full window), St Mary's Church, Fairford

(described by the young Daniel Defoe in his book *The Storm*, published in 1704) which caused severe damage, especially to the three windows of the west wall. Further injury was inflicted in the 19th century when Chance Brothers of Smethwick, Birmingham, were commissioned to restore two lights from the south aisle (depicting Saints Thaddeus and Matthias) and then the upper tier of the Great West Window. Their 'restoration' involved the wholesale removal and replacement of original medieval glass (some of which later found its way to the Victoria and Albert Museum – accession numbers C.12-2004 and C.13-2004) with new, painted copies.[8, 9]

Given this history, Keith was very aware that renewing sections of the windows was a significant undertaking and understood why people might feel apprehensive. However, he was certain that if the heads of Christ and the two thieves in the east window crucifixion scene remained vacant, the emotion of Christ's suffering and that of the thieves was lost. Given the experience and expertise he had gained from projects such as Stanford on Avon, Keith was sure that a well-researched and carefully considered restoration would be of value in recreating the emotional impact of the message. 'I appreciate we will never know the exact portrayal of the lost heads but our attempts to capture the freedom and expression seen in the original painting was by careful study of the existing details. We also knew the two thieves, as they are depicted elsewhere in the scheme; being led to the crucifixion, one is bearded and the other clean shaven. We stylised the head of the repentant thief on that of St John comforting Mary. The grimacing expression of the impenitent thief was taken from the scene of Christ carrying the cross.'

Images of Christ elsewhere in the scheme also provided vital information for recreating his face. 'The head of Christ is almost an exact mirror image of Christ in the flagellation portrayal. We know that he would have been wearing the crown of thorns, as seen in the deposition window' (fig.1.5b). Keith was supported in these endeavours by both art-historical advice from Professor Richard Marks and by talented glass-painters, including Harry Harvey[10] and Helen Whittaker.

The success of Barley Studio's restoration work was noted both by the parish and the wider authorities including English Heritage:

> The figures of Christ and the two thieves have been executed with imagination and great sensitivity, and the repair, cleaning and removal of break leads make the whole work so very much easier for the visitor to understand.[11]

> It was a great pleasure to view the successful restoration of the east window . . . What a transformation! I found the window for the first time entirely legible, lucent and indeed a worthy culmination and focus for your magnificent collection of glass.[12]

For Keith, the satisfaction lies in knowing that, thanks to their conservation, restoration and environmental protection, the windows will now survive and continue to be treasured for generations to come. His fascination with the windows and the original artists and craftspeople behind the Fairford scheme formed the basis of his Masters by Research awarded by the University of York in 2015.[13]

Keith continues to hold fast to his belief that 'if we are to honour the intentions of the original donors, designers, artists and craftsmen, we should, wherever possible through expert collaboration undertake well executed restoration, and well documented, reversible intervention'.

Alongside his own work with historic glass, Keith shared his studio facilities with the renowned stained-glass artist Harry Harvey, often leading and installing his new windows. With Harry, he recognised the importance of good draughtsmanship in design work, and the ways in which the craft supports the art, experimenting with leadlines to shape the design in stained glass. 'A successful window is one in which the intentions of the designer are sympathetically and sensitively interpreted by the craftsman ensuring that the technical aspects contribute to the artistic impact of the finished window.'

SOUTHWELL MINSTER, NOTTINGHAMSHIRE

In 1996, Keith was invited to collaborate with architect Martin Stancliffe and stained-glass artist Patrick Reyntiens[14] on the creation of the Great West Window, Southwell Minster, Nottinghamshire (figs 1.6a and 1.6b). Keith was able to bring his knowledge of the materials and structures used by earlier craftsmen to advise Patrick on suitable glass, paint and stain colours that would typically have been used in the 'golden age' of 15th-century stained glass within this Perpendicular stonework.

Soon afterwards, Helen Whittaker joined the Barley Studio team. Keith notes that 'Helen's early experience of working on restoration painting for Fairford is reflected in many of her own designs, with her interests in narrative, geometry and painting style.' Following the collaboration with Stancliffe and Reyntiens for Southwell Minster, Barley Studio was commissioned to create 16 new windows for its north and south transepts, with Helen as the artist. Helen's timeless geometric design uses subtle tints of glass in keeping with this 12th-century historic building (fig.1.7).

Over the past 50 years, Keith and Barley Studio have been instrumental in challenging the accepted ethics of conservation and restoration, and in developing innovative ways to preserve stained glass. Stained-glass conservation continues to be critiqued and developed, although collaboration between craftspeople, artists and scholars is now common practice. As Sarah Brown, Director of the York Glaziers Trust, has commented:

The sensitive approach to the balance between conservation and restoration achieved by Barley Studio at Stanford on Avon and Fairford revealed to many the capacity of stained-glass conservation to transform public engagement with the medium.

Both projects also highlighted the importance of collaboration between conservators and scholars, an approach very much in step with the way we now work at the York Glaziers Trust.'[15]

Keith's commitment to ensuring future generations can enjoy the beauty of ancient glass continues to this day. 'I have been privileged in working on historic stained glass of all periods during my career. My passion and desire has always been to treat every stained-glass window as a work of art rather than merely an object of antiquity; respecting their imagery, meaning, and above all the intentions of the original artist.'

1.6a   Patrick Reyntiens and Barley Studio, detail of Great West Window, 1996, stained glass, 650 × 1150 cm, Southwell Minster

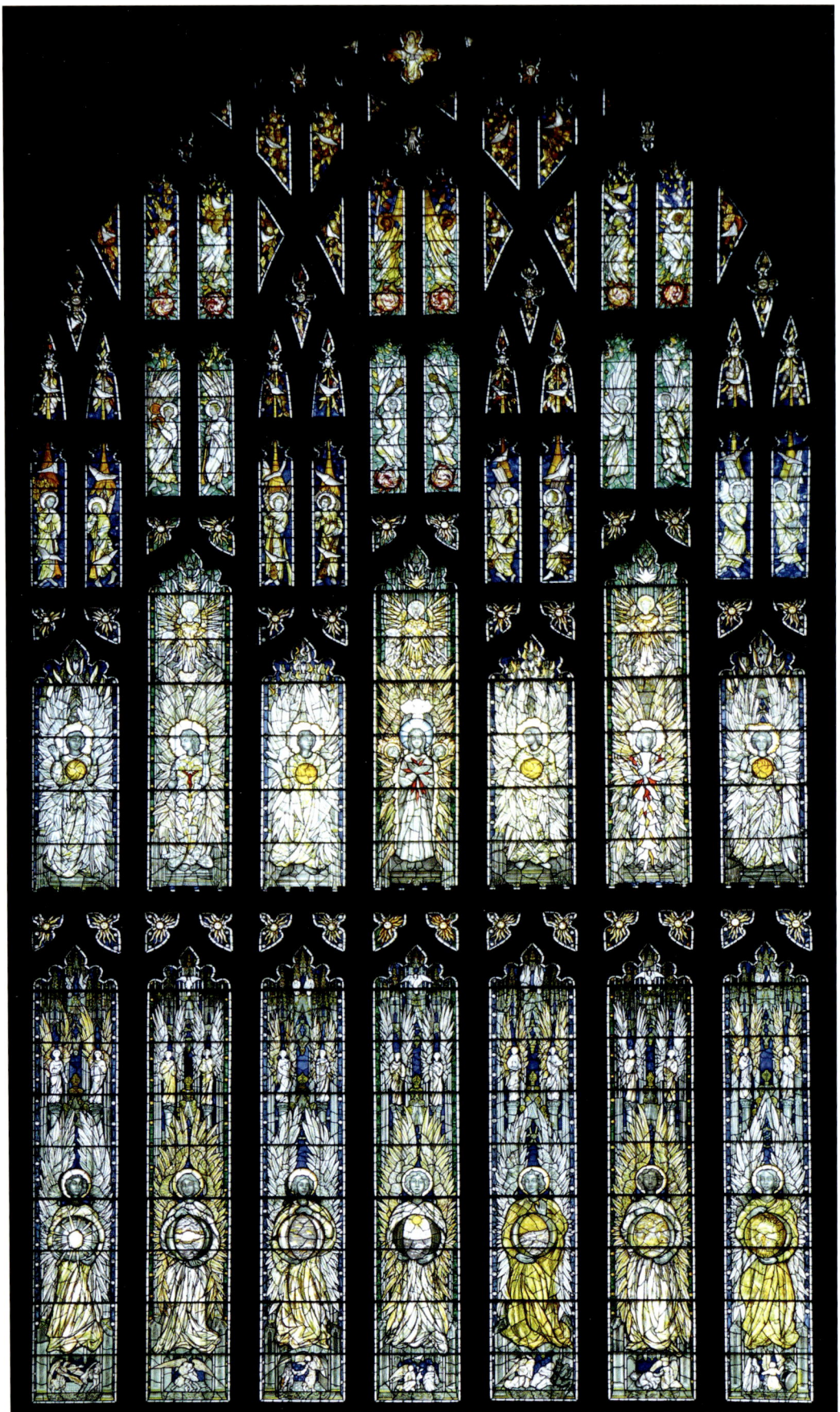

2.1a *St Cuthbert*, 2003, stained glass, 190 × 500 cm, Great West Window, Worksop Priory

2

CREATIVITY AND CRAFT

Helen Whittaker MBE, Creative Director of Barley Studio, has been designing stained glass for the past 30 years. One of her chief aims is to ensure that this treasured art and craft continues to be visible as an art form. She works to promote awareness of the discipline by engaging with funding bodies and business leaders, and by supporting stained-glass competitions such as the Stevens Architectural Glass Competition, organised by the Worshipful Company of Glaziers and Painters of Glass. Helen was a member of the jury for the Stevens competition from 2006 to 2016 and has been Chair of the jury since 2016. In addition, she leads international and national workshops and delivers lectures to members of the general public and professional colleagues to promote engagement with this beautiful and inspiring craft.

For Helen, it is essential to use her design concepts to explore how new ideas and innovative practice might be embedded alongside older perspectives and practices to direct and nourish the genre. 'I aim to achieve a balance which is respectful of the tradition whilst connecting to contemporary art practices and culture.' Her knowledge of medieval illumination, figurative painting and decorative art has its roots in art classes at school where she was encouraged to develop her interest in a wide range of narrative approaches and the emotional intentions found in many paintings. In her undergraduate degree in Three-dimensional Glass and Ceramics at the University of Sunderland (1993–6), Helen acquired skills in the craft of creating stained glass: how to select appropriate colours, work with lead calme, and play with the translucency of the glass using paint in order to use light to bring her designs to life.

'The process of creating stained glass was important to me as I realised that, rather than achieving an immediate result as in painting, there were stages to follow which gave me a chance to reflect and adapt the thought process to achieve the desired end result. The real thrill is in finding ways to bring new ideas and approaches to window design and creation in innovative and spontaneous ways.'

This sense of curiosity was nurtured by Professor Keith Critchlow[1] who directed the Visual Islamic and Traditional Arts (VITA) programme at the Prince of Wales Institute of Architecture (now the King's Foundation) where Helen completed a Master's degree (1996–8). Studying the influential and thought-provoking works of writers such as Plato and Dionysius the Areopagite at VITA gave Helen a deeper understanding of the spiritual aspect of her creative work.

Critchlow introduced Helen to a range of traditional arts and ideas from around the world, and encouraged her to closely examine medieval Christian imagery and translate it into glass. 'Critchlow's thinking provided me with new ways to look at, and think about, the medieval world's art and architecture, particularly Chartres Cathedral, and how it related to us and to the cosmos. I was encouraged to bring my artistic freedom, drawing by eye and then to support this with the discipline of geometric principles inherent in the construction of artworks and buildings from the past.' These approaches provided a strong foundation for Helen's ongoing creative practice.

Helen believes that every commission brings its own possibilities and demands its own individual approach, in design style and execution.

left

left

2.1b   Detail of head of St Cuthbert, 2003, stained glass, Worksop Priory

right

2.1c   *St Cuthbert*, vignette of lantern signalling the saint's death, 2003, stained glass, Worksop Priory

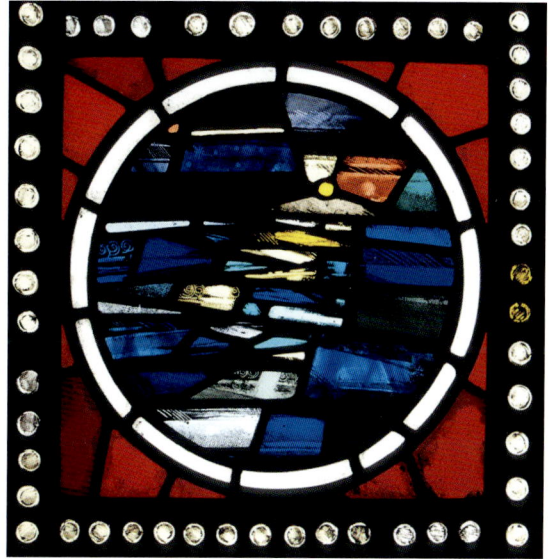

The following commissions highlight the variety of approaches Helen uses to convey and strengthen the visual message of her artwork, from surface treatments of glass and the incorporation of mixed media to the use of bold lettering.

WORKSOP PRIORY, NOTTINGHAMSHIRE

The brief for Helen's window for Worksop Priory, Nottinghamshire, was to create a standing figure in keeping with the Romanesque architecture of the Priory (fig.2.1a). 'I decided to use the Tickhill Psalter, a 14th-century illustrated manuscript which had originally been in Worksop Priory, as my inspiration.' Helen used traditional glass paints, fired onto the glass to create the detail of the picture, such as the face of St Cuthbert (fig.2.1b) and the otters at his feet. Her painting is contemporary and naturalistic, rather than being typically Romanesque. The vignettes in the border, in keeping with medieval narrative convention, tell stories from the life of St Cuthbert, such as the news of his death being signalled by lantern to the watchers at

Lindisfarne (fig.2.1c). In this small square, the story is told in an abstract format, with fragments of glass being used to represent the sea, rather than painting a seascape. 'Through this combination of medieval illumination, realistic painting and abstracted use of glass, I met the brief but I also incorporated my own contemporary vision within the design.'

BEVERLEY MINSTER, EAST YORKSHIRE

In 2003, The Friends of Beverley Minster were concerned that the Minster might become more a museum than a space for active spiritual contemplation and reflection. They held a national competition for new artwork for the 13th-century retro-quire, the site of St John of Beverley's shrine. The brief was to represent 21st-century pilgrimage in an innovative way to help reinvigorate the Minster as a focus of dynamic spiritual culture.

'I recognised this commission as an opportunity to expand my own practice by thinking beyond a 2D window and its frame. I decided that the theme "pilgrimage" could only be fully met by physical movement through, and interaction with, the entire space of the retro-quire.' Helen's scheme comprises four components: a six-metre-high, single lancet stained-glass window; two life-sized figures sculpted from triangles of copper with 'hearts' of glass; a candle stand; and oak benches and kneelers for meditation and prayer (figs 2.2a–2.2e).

'I used the juxtaposition of geometric shapes incorporated in all of the components of the work as a way of guiding the "pilgrim" through the space. The scheme in Beverley Minster expands from the heart of the window, representing God the creator.' In *Pilgrimage* it is the viewer's decision where they begin: with the lighting of a candle that takes them on a journey to the window, or with the patterns and colours of the glass in the window.

Pilgrimage was a pivotal moment in Helen's thinking and practice, and it influenced a number of commissions where spatial and artistic approaches have been combined to guide viewers physically and metaphorically. As her first large-scale sculptural work, Helen enlisted the expertise of renowned sculptor Harold Gosney,[2] who has continued to act as a consultant for many of her three-dimensional projects.

right

2.2a *Pilgrimage*, 2004, stained glass,
600 × 200 cm, retro-quire, Beverley Minster

far right

2.2b *Pilgrimage*, 2004, two life-size sculpted pilgrims in copper, retro-quire, Beverley Minster

overleaf

2.2c Helen Whittaker cutting glass for the *Pilgrimage* window, 2004, Barley Studio, Dunnington, York

2.2d   Keith Barley working on life-size
sculpted pilgrims in copper, 2004, Barley
Studio, Dunnington, York

2.2e *Pilgrimage*, votive candle stand with sculpted figures and prayer kneelers, 2004, copper and oak, retro-quire, Beverley Minster

ST MARY'S CHURCH, LOCKINGTON, EAST YORKSHIRE

Helen's window for St Mary's Church, Lockington, York is based on the parable of the sower from Luke's Gospel, and the verse 'Some fell into good soil'.[3] The clients wanted plenty of light to flow through the window without obscuring the view of the surrounding countryside. 'The constraints of this narrow window provided me with an opportunity to tell this story in a more abstract way through colour and text. I created a central focus to the window using deep blue and yellow, suggesting the sky and a wheat field.'

The arrangement of the letters of the text itself creates the picture which tells the story: the letters of 'some' are like the seed leaving the sower's hand; the letters in 'fell' fall downwards towards the bottom of the window; 'into' intersects the wheat field; and 'good' and 'soil' are at the base of the image in the roots of the wheat. The leadwork was designed to emphasise the rhythm of this design, with the semi-vertical zig-zag pattern following the movement of the words (figs 2.3a and 2.3b).

2.4 *The Paradise Window*, 2014, stained glass, 400 × 490 cm, east window,
St Brandon's Church, Brancepeth, Durham

ST BRANDON'S CHURCH, BRANCEPETH, DURHAM

The interior of the medieval church of St Brandon, Brancepeth, Durham was destroyed in a fire in 1998. The intent of the restoration was to create a light and contemporary ambience in the space. 'There were two conflicting wishes for the replacement window: one to re-create a fully coloured stained-glass window with a Christian message, the other to use clear-etched glazing to be able to view the verdant landscape outside the building. I was keen to find a design solution to resolve this dilemma to meet both needs.' The original window had focused on the church's namesake St Brandon who, according to legend, had sailed away to find the Garden of Eden. With this in mind Helen created a design using large pieces of glass which fills the top half of the window, creating an explosion of large-scale, vibrant flora 'announcing' St Brandon's arrival in Eden: hibiscus and a cluster of jacaranda flowers. Unusually for a stained-glass window, the glass in the lower half of the design is left clear so that the natural landscape of the exterior can be seen from within the church (fig.2.4).

ST THOMAS OF CANTERBURY CHURCH, GREATFORD, LINCOLNSHIRE

At St Thomas of Canterbury Church in Greatford, Lincolnshire, Helen was commissioned to create stained glass for the last remaining clear glass window. 'The brief asked for a non-figurative representation of the saint and also requested reference to the 12th-century Becket reliquary, held in the Victoria and Albert Museum, London. I used Becket's highly decorated "apparel of the amice", in the collection of Sens Cathedral, to form the dividing element between the "earthly" and "heavenly" realms of the window. Details from the Becket reliquary inspired the heavens above.'

At the base of the window, three choughs (from Becket's coat of arms) are flying over the watercress fields and reed beds of the River Glen around Greatford. Their zig-zag shape draws the eye upwards to the central motif of the window (fig.2.5).

2.5 *The Becket Window*, 2015, stained glass, 110 × 280 cm, south nave window, St Thomas' Church, Greatford

2.6 *The Parable of the Sower* (lettering by Phil Thomas), 2018, stained glass, 120 × 230 cm, north nave aisle, St Mary Magdalene, Hart, Hartlepool

In order to create the intricate patterns of the amice, Helen used stains and enamels to achieve multiple transparent colours on the glass without the division of lead. The entire design is framed within clear, diamond quarries to allow natural light in. Both light and colourful, the bold nature of the design is intended to emphasise the strength of Becket's character and highlight the drama of his martyrdom.

ST MARY MAGDALENE, HART, HARTLEPOOL, COUNTY DURHAM

At St Mary Magdalene, Hart, Helen was asked to create a non-figurative version of the parable of the sower. In response Helen composed a vortex of seeds scattering from the Sower's hand, with poppies and wheat intersected by rocky soil, and sparrows pecking at the seed. The wheat is created through abundant use of yellow stain, with minimal leadlines accentuating the feeling of movement through the window.

At the heart of the vortex sits a 'window' of blue, with the dove symbolising the Holy Spirit rising up within it. The motion of the vortex is intended to pull the viewer into a closer engagement with the central message of God's gifts of creation and the cycle of nature (fig.2.6).

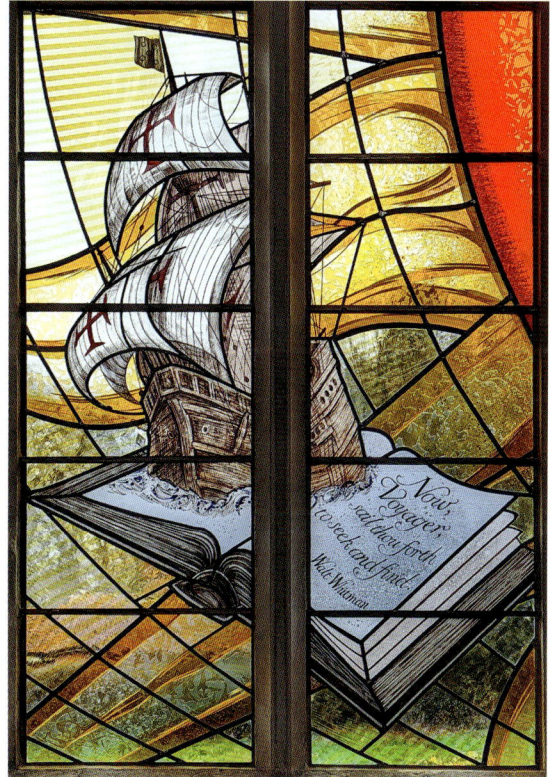

2.7a *Axis Mundi* (lettering by Tracey Sheppard), detail of left window, 2023, stained glass, 180 × 380 cm, north nave aisle, All Saints Church, Wetheringsett cum Brockford

ALL SAINTS CHURCH, WETHERINGSETT, SUFFOLK

The English geographer Richard Hakluyt (1552–1616) was also Rector of All Saints Church, Wetheringsett, Suffolk. This provided the starting point for Helen's design for two Perpendicular-style three-light windows in adjacent bays of the north wall of the church. The surrounding windows are traditional clear, quarry-glazed windows. 'I wanted this design to be viewed as a whole, despite the span of wall between them, with sufficient light and luminosity to blend with its clear counterparts.'

The overall circular structure of the design linking the two windows is derived from Abraham Ortelius' *Theatrum Orbis Terrarum* of 1570, widely regarded as the first modern atlas and a work which Hakluyt probably knew. Helen designed one window to represent Wetheringsett and the local farming community and the other to depict migration to far-off lands. The Walt Whitman quotation, 'Now Voyager sail thou forth to seek and find',[4] included in the design emphasises the fulfilment of travel. Helen made much use of plating and acid etching in the design to create texture and to allow it to sparkle while ensuring a good balance of light with the neighbouring windows (figs 2.7a and 2.7b).

overleaf

2.7b *Axis Mundi* (lettering by Tracey Sheppard), 2023, stained glass, 180 × 380 cm, north nave aisle, All Saints Church, Wetheringsett cum Brockford

O give
thanks
unto the
Lord,
for he
is good,
for his mercy
endureth
for ever

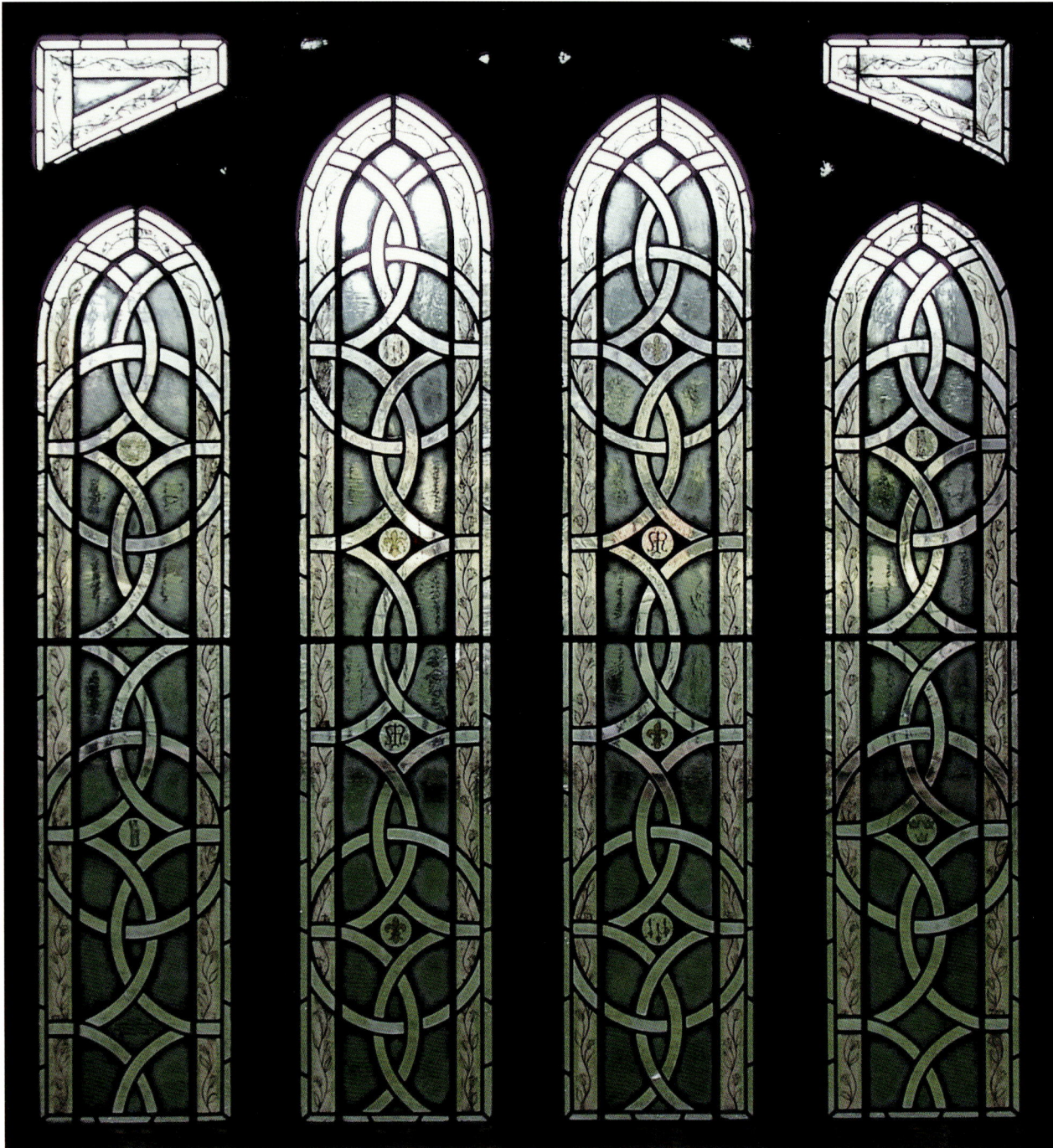

3.1a   The *New Processional Way*, detail of four lights, 2000, stained glass, 166 × 180 cm, Ely Cathedral

3
CONCEPT TO CREATION

Stained-glass windows are often thought of as the output of a single designer (as the designer often includes their signature on the work). However, there is usually a collaborative element, with glass painters and glaziers often assisting in the process to ensure the realisation of the commission.

As a stained-glass artist, it is Helen's responsibility to consider each step of the process from initial concept to fully realised creation, completed with the support of the Barley Studio team. When designing a window Helen strives to create an individual and meaningful response to each commission: 'I like to break down the perceived expectations of what a stained-glass window should or could be. My aim is to engage the viewer with my work so that, rather than just look and quickly pass by, the onlooker might consider what they can see in front of them and question what the work might mean to them as an artwork, a story or a moment of spiritual reflection.'

Helen always refers to key points to drive the process, from the concept, to the creation of the design, through to the translation into the glass itself. 'I relish the opportunity to create a convincing image in response to the client, the brief and the building.'

The history and architectural style of the building itself and the context within which the architecture is set have to be taken into account. The shape and style of the architectural opening for the window and the complexity of the stone mullions and the supporting metalwork to the window have to be explored. The light levels within the space at different times are profoundly important, as are the existing artworks which will be seen in conjunction with the design. The purpose of the window and the users of the building are also integral to these initial considerations of the design. Reflecting on these points influences the approach that Helen takes in crafting a narrative that respects the client's wishes, the needs of the brief and the use of the building. This in turn informs the style of Helen's artwork – whether figurative, abstract or symbolic – and the chosen imagery. 'My aim is to engage the viewer through good design and craftsmanship, creating energy and movement intertwining contemporary and traditional elements. I believe that new stained-glass windows should be respectful of their surroundings, while also engaging the viewer to guide them on their emotional or artistic journey.'

Helen's creative process begins with a vidimus (small-scale design) created either by hand or digitally, which is then developed into a full-size cartoon. From that a cutline is created, and the selected glass is cut to size, treated and fired to create texture and depth. The glass is then set within the lead matrix following the cutline and made waterproof, ready for installation. 'This is an evolving creative process which must be constantly reviewed at each stage to ensure a successful outcome.'

THE *NEW PROCESSIONAL WAY*, ELY CATHEDRAL, CAMBRIDGESHIRE

The brief for the *New Processional Way*, Ely Cathedral's Millennium Project, was to create a scheme of windows in a new passageway – created by Jane Kennedy, then architect at Ely Cathedral – following a route once taken by medieval monks from the body of the cathedral to the Lady Chapel.

3.1b The *New Processional Way*, 2000, stained glass, detail of three windows, each 180 × 190 cm, and two lights, each 20 × 190 cm, Ely Cathedral

The requirement was for the windows to echo 14th-century grisaille glazing and to enhance the newly created corridor. 'I created a scheme of interlocking circles, which continued along the entire scheme. Simplicity of colour and design created a seamless sense of flow along the space as it transitions from one building to another.' The design incorporates small circular motifs with symbols relating to Ely Cathedral and the Virgin Mary, surrounded by a decorative border of lilies (figs 3.1a and 3.1b).

ST ETHELBURGA'S CENTRE FOR RECONCILIATION AND PEACE, BISHOPSGATE, LONDON

On 24 April 1993, the 15th-century church of St Ethelburga in Bishopsgate, London, was almost completely destroyed by a bomb. Only the east end of the building remained, including the medieval support structure (ferramenta) and some fragmentary remains of the 1872 Charles Eamer Kempe east window.

Nine years later, the restored building reopened as a centre for reconciliation and peace to encourage faith communities to work together. As part of the rebuild, a new east window was commissioned by Bishop Richard Chartres, then Bishop of London, to reflect the history of the building and its new purpose.

One important element of this project was the surviving ferramenta, which cast heavy shadows through the window. Helen's response was to use intense painting and leading to ensure the original ironwork was obscured when viewed from inside the building. In the window, St Ethelburga, shown as a Benedictine abbess, strides across the composition, eyes fixed on a radiant vision of a heavenly Jerusalem, her cloak billowing behind her with the upward sweep of the cloth revealing a kaleidoscope of coloured glass fragments (fig.3.2). These fragments were salvaged from Kempe's 1872 window. The process of salvaging and recycling older glass is not new, but it was imbued with particular importance here, acknowledging the history of the site and contributing to the optimism of the newly created centre.

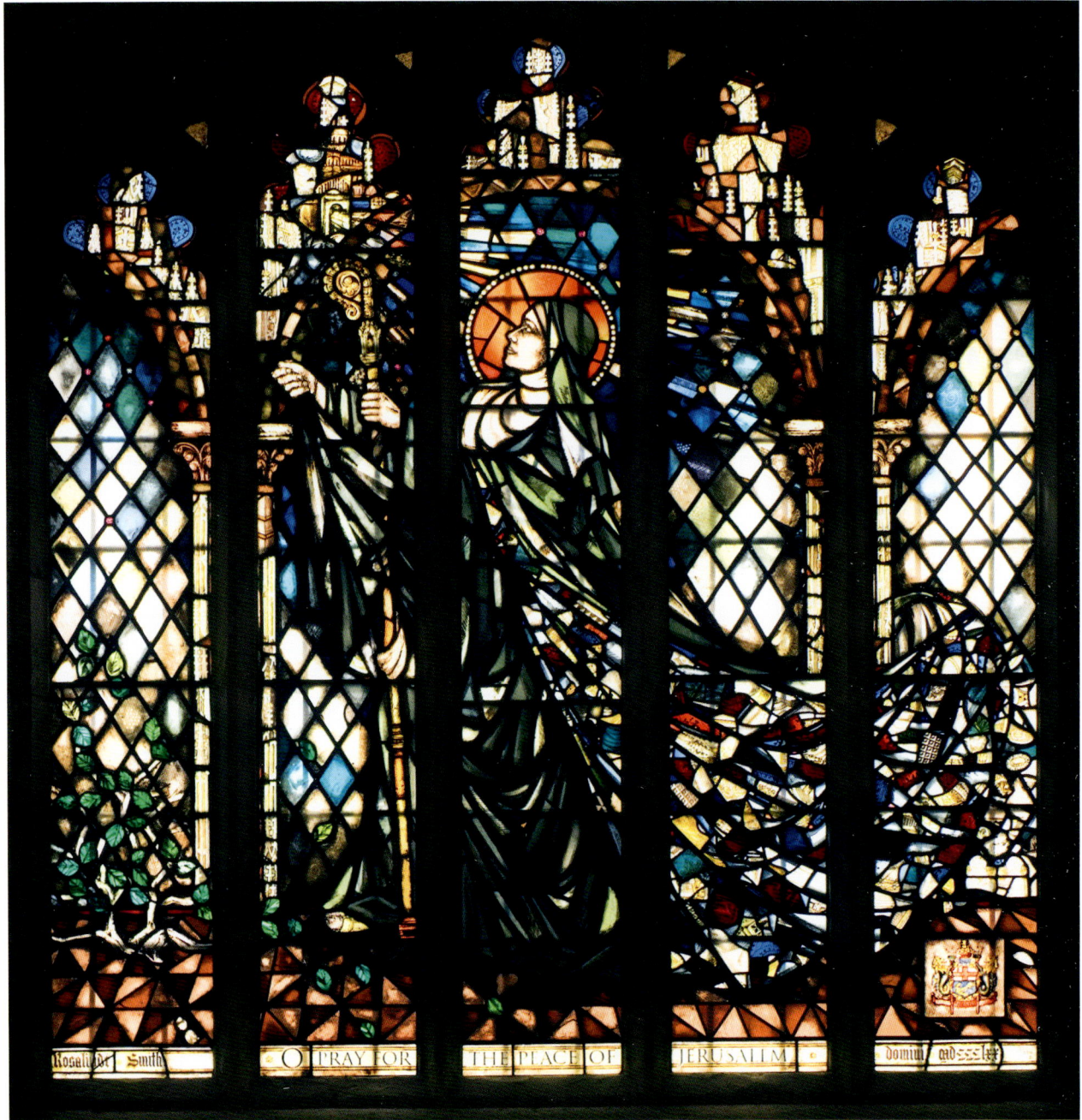

3.2 *St Ethelburga*, 2002, stained glass, 330 × 330 cm, east window, St Ethelburga's
Centre for Reconciliation and Peace, Bishopsgate, London

3.3a *The Four Seasons*, 2005–6, Helen Whittaker painting detail of spring,
stained glass, 190 × 400 cm, Barley Studio, Dunnington, York

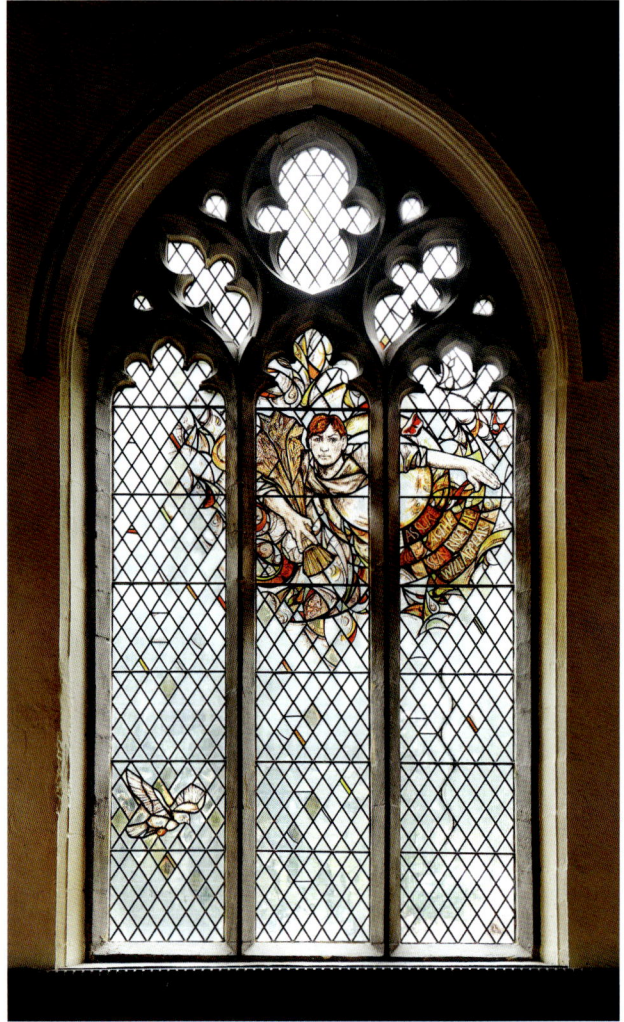

ST PETER AND ST MARY'S CHURCH, STOWMARKET, SUFFOLK

'For this commission at St Peter and St Mary's Church, Stowmarket, Suffolk, I was asked to create a design incorporating the four seasons in recognition of the donor's farming heritage. I also had to accommodate the varying Decorated-style stonework of each window and find a way to create a coherent design. Since the windows are in the south side of the church with intense light, I chose to work mostly in monochrome with just a few touches of colour in the design.' The four seasons have been a recurring theme for stained-glass designers, used to remind the viewer of God's creation, of the passing of time and the transition from new beginnings to endings. In her design Helen associated the seasons with the elements of water (spring), fire (summer),

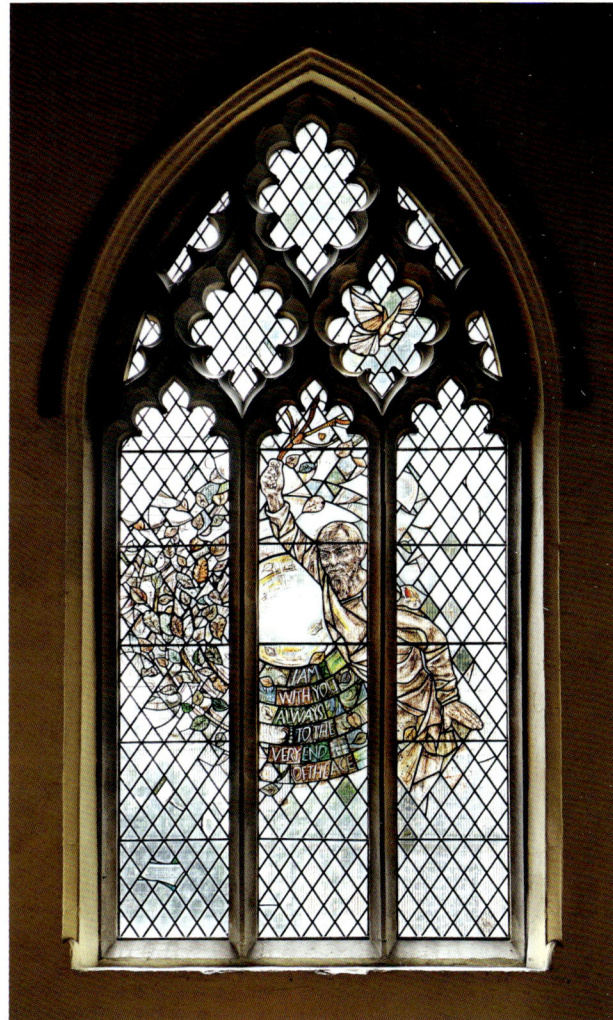

earth (autumn) and air (winter). The figurative vignettes in each three-light window are placed at different heights to create a sense of movement and flow across the entire scheme as one season leads to another. Each image is subtly defined through colour to match the elements and seasons. The figures in the windows age according to the season, from the youth of spring to the old age of winter (figs 3.3a and 3.3b).

3.3b *The Four Seasons* (lettering by Charles Smith, FRSA), 2005–6, stained glass, 190 × 400 cm, St Peter and St Mary's Church, Stowmarket

ST GREGORY'S CHURCH, KIRKNEWTON, NORTHUMBERLAND

The Parish Church Council of St Gregory's Church, Kirknewton, commissioned a memorial window to honour Josephine Butler's life and her devotion to St Catherine of Siena. Josephine's grave in St Gregory's Church faces a small window in the building's south porch, the chosen site for this memorial.

Josephine Butler (1828–1906) actively campaigned for social reforms in 19th-century Britain. She also wrote a biography of St Catherine of Siena (1347–80), who devoted her life to calling for reform to help those who were ill or lived in poverty.

Helen chose to commemorate Josephine through her words describing St Catherine: 'she loved – she prayed – she endured'. Helen was also keen to use sculpture to further enhance the design. 'I overlaid the slender window with nine copper lilies entwined with bindweed.' The bindweed symbolises the social constraints of

above

3.4a   Memorial to the social reformer Josephine Butler (lettering by Charles Smith, FRSA), 2006, stained glass, 20 × 170 cm, and copper sculpture, 980 sq cm, south porch, St Gregory's Church, Kirknewton

right

3.4b   Memorial to the social reformer Josephine Butler, detail, sculpture in brass and copper, 2006, south porch, St Gregory's Church, Kirknewton

women in Butler's time, and the lilies, symbols of hope, are also associated with St Catherine of Siena. Through the inclusion of the three-dimensional sculptural foliage and flowers, the once overlooked window is now clearly signalled and Josephine's legacy has become a prominent feature of this space (figs 3.4a and 3.4b).

THE ROYAL AIR FORCE CLUB, LONDON

The Royal Air Force Club, London, held a competition to design a new stained-glass window for their staircase, to celebrate 90 years of the RAF and the Club in 2008. The commission presented a number of design challenges in terms of the span of time and events to be represented, the multi-level viewing perspectives from the staircase as well as broad variations in the availability of natural light due to the close proximity of adjacent buildings.

Helen's design, to the brief by Group Captain Tony Banks and Wing Commander Michael Gilbert, illustrates the history of both the Royal Air Force and the RAF Club since their formation in April 1918. The imagery guides the viewer's attention from the bottom of the window rising diagonally upwards, before coming to rest on the circular design in the upper arch. The circle gives reference to both radar and, in a more abstract sense, the moon, giving guidance to the aircraft below (fig.3.5a).

The issue of light variance was particularly challenging at the base of the window, which sees almost no daylight. To compensate for this, Helen decided to employ reflected light from the interior, by gilding the glass (a technique based on 'Verre Églomisé').[1]

The original frame of the Georgian window was kept in place, as well as the extant glass, as Helen felt that their removal would have diminished the overall integrity of the window's relationship to the building. The new stained glass is set in manganese bronze frames and fitted in front of the existing clear glazing, which offers an outer protective layer (figs 3.5b and 3.5c).

3.5a *RAF, Past and Present*, 2008, staircase window, stained glass, 240 × 610 cm, Royal Air Force Club, Piccadilly, London

left

3.5b *RAF, Past and Present*, 2008, view of staircase window, stained glass,
240 × 610 cm, Royal Air Force Club, Piccadilly, London

above

3.5c *RAF, Past and Present*, 2008, detail of staircase window,
stained glass, Royal Air Force Club, Piccadilly, London

3.6a *Pilgrimage*, 2008, two copper sculptures, stained glass and copper, 300 × 650 cm, and 200 cm, east window, St Mary's Church, Bramall Lane, Sheffield

3.6b *Pilgrimage*, 2008, detail, stained glass, St Mary's Church, Bramall Lane, Sheffield

ST MARY'S CHURCH, COMMUNITY AND CONFERENCE CENTRE, SHEFFIELD

Helen was approached by Canon Julian Sullivan of St Mary's Church, Community and Conference Centre in Sheffield to create a combination of glass and sculpture, based on Psalm 84 ('How lovely is your dwelling place'). St Mary's Church shares much of its space with a community centre, with the east end reserved for liturgical events, so the brief was to make this part of the space stand out as a site of spiritual enrichment.

'Given the complex patterns created by the Perpendicular-style stone mullions I knew that a simple design for the window would not be a suitable solution. Instead, I opted for an abstracted pattern formed from many small pieces of glass which, when put together, formed layers of movement, or rhythm, across the entire fenestration.' In the window, abstracted figures representing pilgrims are shown in the lower part of the window as they make their way towards the orb of light in the upper section.

The two copper figures either side of the window were inspired by stone figures from Chartres Cathedral, and are intended to encourage prayer and contemplation, in keeping with the message found in Psalm 84. The figures are sculpted from triangles of copper, representing the Trinity, and forming a link with the shards of glass in the window (figs 3.6a–3.6d). The realistic depiction of the figures creates an identifiable link to the people using the building, both as a church and a community centre. The left hand of the copper figure to the left of the window is raised to guide the viewer's gaze to the pilgrims within the window, whilst the hands of the figure on the right side are crossed in a meditative pose. The complete scheme of artworks aims to remind the viewer of the central tenets of a holy pilgrimage: faith and love.

right

3.6c   *Pilgrimage*, 2008, life-size sculpted pilgrim, copper, St Mary's Church, Bramall Lane, Sheffield

left

3.6d   Helen and the Barley Studio team installing the *Pilgrimage* window, 2008, St Mary's Church, Bramall Lane, Sheffield

right

3.7   Commemorative window to those who served in Afghanistan, 2015, stained glass, 180 × 300 cm, north nave aisle, All Saints Church, Pavement, York

ALL SAINTS CHURCH, PAVEMENT, YORK

All Saints Church, Pavement, York, is the Regimental Church of the Royal Dragoon Guards. Funding for this commission was raised through an appeal organised by *The York Press* in 2013 to commemorate the lives of all who had died or been injured in the Afghan conflict. Helen met with the families of three men who had died in the conflict to understand more about their wishes for the message of the window: the value of being a part of a team, the importance of remembrance, and the hope that the deaths and injuries suffered by all in the conflict would not be in vain. The colours in the window refer to the three regiments of the York servicemen who had died. The pavement spiralling up to a dove (as a symbol of peace) also recalls the identity of All Saints Church as it stands on one of the earliest paved streets in York. The paving stones represent those who participated in active service in the conflict (fig.3.7).

3.8 *Prayer Tree*, 2019, sculpture, glass and
copper, 100 × 170 cm, Multi-Faith Chapel,
Scarborough Hospital

SCARBOROUGH HOSPITAL CHAPEL, EAST YORKSHIRE

'In my commission for the multi-faith chapel at Scarborough Hospital I needed to find a way of creating an accessible work which could be viewed from many angles. The chapel is used by patients, their families and hospital staff, so I wanted to ensure that the work engaged the viewer and offered comfort in some way.' The *Prayer Tree* sculpture was a development of Helen's *Prayer Tree* for York Hospital's multi-faith chapel (2007) which featured a copper and glass sculpture of a leaf with green and gold-coloured glass. Sycamore trees have traditionally been used as symbols of strength, protection, tolerance and hope, so for Scarborough Hospital Helen used the shape of a sycamore seed made from copper and brass sheeting and opalescent glass. Set along the 'veins' of the leaf, small hooks hold the written prayers of the visitors to the chapel (fig.3.8).

ST CUTHBERT'S CHURCH, CRAYKE, NORTH YORKSHIRE

The brief for St Cuthbert's Church, Crayke, was to create a standing figure of St Cuthbert, the dedicatee of the church. Helen took inspiration from the elaborately illuminated Lindisfarne Gospels, closely associated with veneration of the saint. Helen was keen to capture the exceptional artistry of this manuscript, with its bright colours and incredible detail. Her skill in translating a design from one art form to another was essential to the success of this design, with its complex knotwork and detailed decoration. 'Developing my idea of the standing figure I created for the St Cuthbert window at Worksop, I chose to frame the saint with a letter "C" for Cuthbert and also for Crayke, to highlight the importance of the saint and the church's mission of spreading the word of Christianity' (figs 3.9a–3.9c).

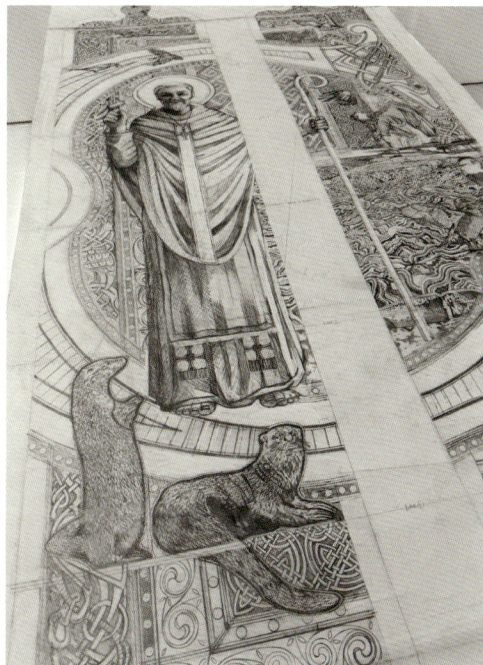

3.9a   *St Cuthbert*, 2020, full-size cartoon, pencil, 110 × 250 cm, Barley Studio, Dunnington, York

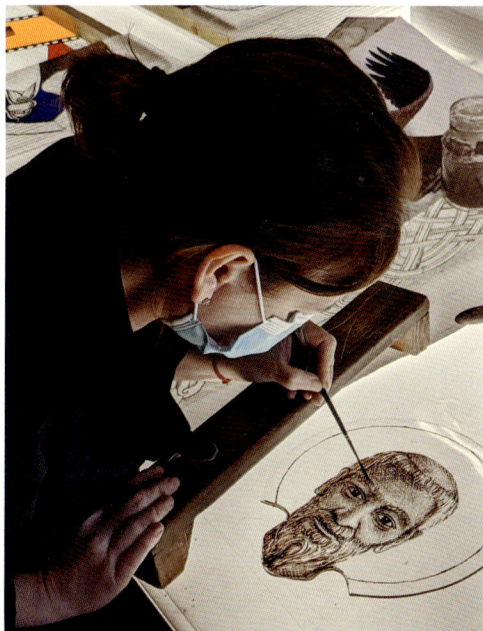

3.9b   Helen Whittaker painting head of St Cuthbert, 2020, 110 × 250 cm, Barley Studio, Dunnington, York

DO NOT JUDGE EACH DAY BY
THE HARVEST YOU REAP

BUT BY THE SEEDS
THAT YOU PLANT

left

3.9c *St Cuthbert*, 2020, stained glass,
110 × 250 cm, north nave aisle, St Cuthbert's
Church, Crayke

right

3.10a Window commemorating the D-Day
Landings (lettering by Phil Thomas), 2020,
stained glass, 40 × 160 cm, porch, St Lawrence's
Church, York

ST LAWRENCE'S CHURCH, YORK

At St Lawrence's Church, York, Helen was
commissioned to create a lasting memorial to
the York Normandy Veterans who took part in the
D-Day Landings and the battles to liberate France
during the Second World War. Helen met with the
surviving York veterans who took part in the D-Day
Landings and who continue to meet in this church,
along with their long-time supporter Nick Beilby.

In the centre of the design, two men are seen
waiting inside a landing craft at the point where
the armoured doors are opening and the ramp
is being lowered. The badge on their backpacks
identifies them as City of York Normandy Veterans.
Helen's design aims to capture a moment where
'the lead man turns back to his comrade offering
his support so that they can face the coming assault
together'. It is a dramatic moment in the heat of
the battle. Below the men's feet can be seen images
representing the homes they are defending. 'I
included the motifs of home, along with the words
from the hymn "Judge Eternal", to indicate how
these men must have felt caught between two
worlds, their thoughts moving between the security
of home and the horror of the battle' (figs 3.10a
and 3.10b).

AND THE
HOMESTEADS AND
THE WOODLANDS
PLEAD IN SILENCE
FOR THEIR
PEACE

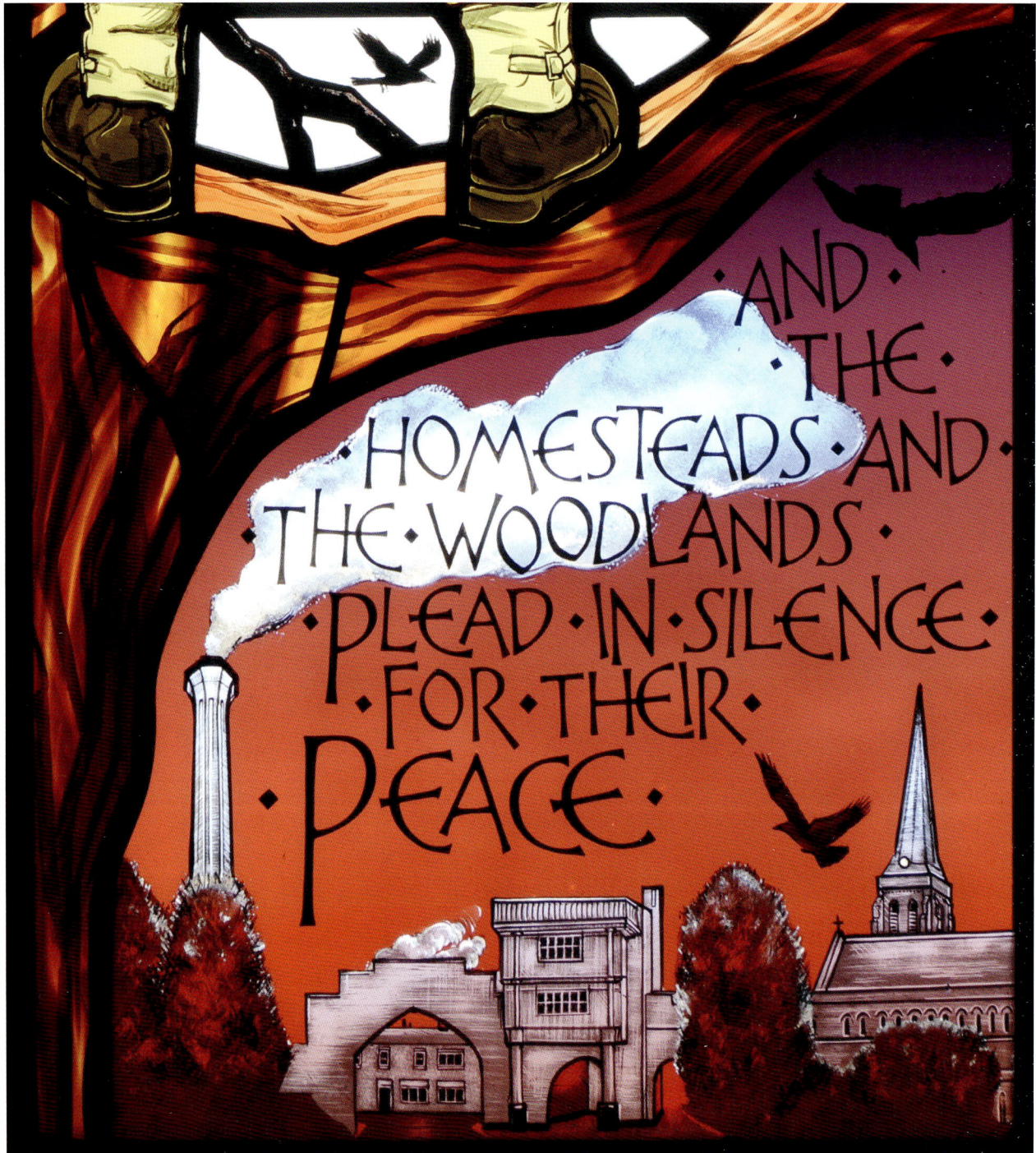

3.10b Window commemorating the D-Day Landings (lettering by Phil Thomas), 2020, detail, stained glass, 40 × 160 cm, porch, St Lawrence's Church, York

4

CHANGE AND CONTINUITY

New generations have always built on ideas and methods from the past, to elaborate, recreate and innovate. A deep understanding of the practical and artistic process of stained glass informs the Barley Studio team's response to conservation, restoration and new work. This belief in combining old and new approaches is at the core of Barley Studio's work and encourages the team to build on its understanding of past designs and processes while embracing new ideas and techniques. Translations from other media, from medieval manuscripts to modern technologies, show the versatility and opportunities of stained glass. At times, a blending of the past and present may occur in the same window, with old and new side by side. This informed approach allows the continuation of the discipline and its evolution for a contemporary audience. The following examples demonstrate the connections Helen's artworks make between past principles and ideas and contemporary thinking and practice.

Helen's first exploration of overtly Christian imagery was an exhibition panel depicting the Tree of Jesse. 'I created this work, which is based on an illuminated page in the Winchester Psalter, to highlight how medieval work could be a stimulus for exploring how to interpret line and colour and adapt it in the traditional medium of stained glass. My panel uses a typical medieval stained-glass palette to emulate the colours and the flat two-dimensional aspects of window designs from the medieval era.' It was the first large-scale panel which Helen created with advice and guidance from Barley Studio. 'Here I learnt about the six colours used by medieval glaziers and I also had the opportunity to

4.1   *Tree of Jesse*, based on the 12th-century *Winchester Psalter*, 1998, stained-glass panel, 90 × 180 cm, Barley Studio, Dunnington, York

left

left

4.2a   East window, 2003, stained glass,
190 × 380 cm, The Priory Church of
St Mary and St Lawrence, Ellerton

right

4.2b   View of the rebuilt Priory Church,
east window, 2003, detail, stained glass,
Ellerton Priory

see medieval glass in detail to better understand
the lead matrix and its role in outlining the design,
bringing strength structurally and artistically. I
could also see the way texture was created and how
this could then manipulate the flow and levels of
light.' In terms of the content of the design, the
original manuscript gave Helen the chance to study
geometric pattern in detail. For *Tree of Jesse* Helen
used a pair of compasses to accurately recreate the
patterned structure as the focus of the work. 'By
doing this I learnt how the various angles created
movement within the overarching composition and
gave a particular energy to the panel' (fig.4.1).

ST MARY AND ST LAWRENCE'S CHURCH, ELLERTON, EAST YORKSHIRE

In 2002, Helen won the commission for the
Stevens Competition, organised by the Worshipful
Company of Glaziers and Painters of Glass. The
brief for a new east window for St Mary and St
Lawrence's Church, Ellerton, East Yorkshire,
requested a response to the landscape and ecology
of Derwent Ings, a nature reserve and Site of
Special Scientific Interest.

The Priory Church had fallen into disuse in the
late 1970s and the contents stripped from it in 1984.
In 1995, the Ellerton Church Preservation Trust was
established in the building as a centre for artistic
and cultural events. 'This commission helped me to
expand my thinking in new ways as the brief did not
require a reference to the original dedicatee of the
church or any specific religious text. This gave me
new-found freedom to explore a narrative from fresh
perspectives.'

Helen took the perspective of a viewer standing in
the ruins of the 13th-century priory looking through
a large red quatrefoil aperture to the rebuilt priory
of the 20th century to create a liminal space where
ideas of time past and present are merged. To extend
this idea, copies of the original coat of arms of the
families who had been associated with Ellerton Priory
in the 14th century were reinserted in the traceries
(figs 4.2a and 4.2b).

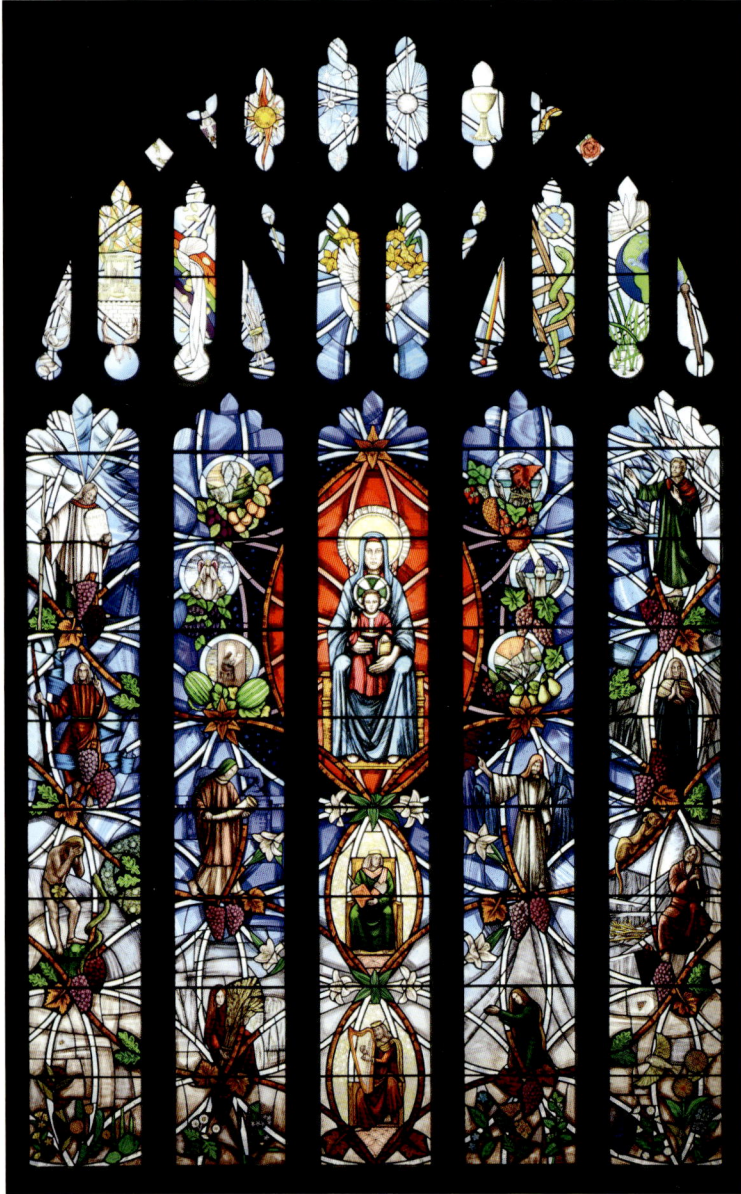

4.3a   The 'Jesse' window and detail of Mary, 2016, stained glass, 360 × 560 cm,
east window of the Lewis Chapel, St Mary's Priory Church, Abergavenny

ST MARY'S PRIORY CHURCH, ABERGAVENNY, MONMOUTHSHIRE

The figurative window at St Mary's Priory Church, Abergavenny was commissioned to complete the story of the late-medieval oak sculpture of Jesse which remains here, and is now directly sited under Helen's new window. Inspired and informed by the ancient iconography and theme, Helen uses geometry echoing that seen in traditional Jesse windows to create the overarching structure of the new design. Overlapping circles, spreading out from the heart of Christ, create the vine branches which provide the framework for the figures of the Virgin and Child, prophets, priests and kings to rest upon.

Helen's window also references Abergavenny, with representations of seven Celtic saints surrounding the Virgin and Child, as well as St Mary's Priory Church, with their 'Advent Jesse' depicted in the tracery. The healing plants of the church's monastic garden are shown at the base of the window. All of the design elements are brought together through its vibrant, rich colours, red, blue and purple highlighting the majesty of the Virgin and Child (figs 4.3a–4.3c).

top

4.3b   Adam, the 'Jesse' window, 2016, detail, stained glass, east window of the Lewis Chapel, St Mary's Priory Church, Abergavenny

bottom

4.3c   St Teilo, the 'Jesse' window, 2016, detail, stained glass, east window of the Lewis Chapel, St Mary's Priory Church, Abergavenny

THE ROYAL AIR FORCE CLUB, PICCADILLY, LONDON

The *Celebrating Women in the RAF* window at the Royal Air Force Club, Piccadilly, London, uniquely combines traditional and contemporary glass imagery and techniques. It was commissioned to honour the bravery and service of all women in the RAF, again led by Group Captain Tony Banks and Wing Commander Michael Gilbert. 'Taking inspiration from the iconic image of the American factory worker, "Rosie the Riveter" I developed the idea of the female worker holding the Air Force together through the fixing of rivets in an aeroplane factory.' This example from Second World War poster art also influenced the bold graphic style of the design, with its strong lines and block colours.

The left window recognises the variety of vital roles women provided to the Royal Air Force in the

First and Second World Wars, both while serving in uniform and as civilians. The window on the right celebrates women who are now fully integrated into operational roles within the Royal Air Force (figs 4.4a–4.4c).

Alongside traditional leaded work, large glass 'rivets', in the form of glass lenses, were set into the window, blending the leaded glass with a layer of screen-printed photographs of women serving

the RAF laid behind. The lines of 'rivets' are set at eye level across the base of the window through which the printed images can be viewed, drawing on historical and contemporary images charting the transformation of the status of women in the RAF.

4.4a *Celebrating Women in the RAF*, 2018, stained glass and sculpture, 410 × 180 cm, The Royal Air Force Club, Piccadilly, London

4.4b *Celebrating Women in the RAF*, 2018, detail of lens, showing historic photo from the RAF past, The Royal Air Force Club, Piccadilly, London

4.4c HRH Queen Elizabeth II viewing *Celebrating Women in the RAF*, 2018, The Royal Airforce Club, Piccadilly, London

WESTMINSTER ABBEY, LONDON

In 2016, David Hockney RA was commissioned by the Dean of Westminster, Dr John Hall, to create a design for a window in Westminster Abbey to celebrate Queen Elizabeth II's reign. 'I was invited to collaborate to help ensure a successful translation of his vision to the very large stained-glass window in the north transept. The Dean's brief was to create a symbolic or representational design which would be recognisably Hockney.'

Hockney created a country scene of blue skies and hawthorn blossom of his native Yorkshire Wolds to reflect Queen Elizabeth's own love of the countryside. His design is stylistically different to the surrounding stained glass, a conscious choice by the artist. Hockney used an iPad to create his design, as he felt that working on an illuminated surface was the natural way to develop a work based in light. He visited Barley Studio to explore the qualities of different kinds of glass, and to understand the materials and technical possibilities. Helen says that 'because the windows were so large, I initially worked with Hockney at half-scale to help take into account the existing support structure of the window. Once enlarged to full-size, I created

4.5a   David Hockney RA and Helen Whittaker working on the half-scale design for *The Queen's Window*, 2018, showing cartoon, Hockney Studio, California

65

left

left

4.5b   David Hockney RA, *The Queen's Window*, 2018, stained glass, 350 × 850 cm, west wall transept, Westminster Abbey, London

right

4.6a   Memorial window to the Worsley family (lettering by Phil Thomas), 2020, stained glass, 100 × 200 cm, north nave aisle, All Saints Church, Hovingham

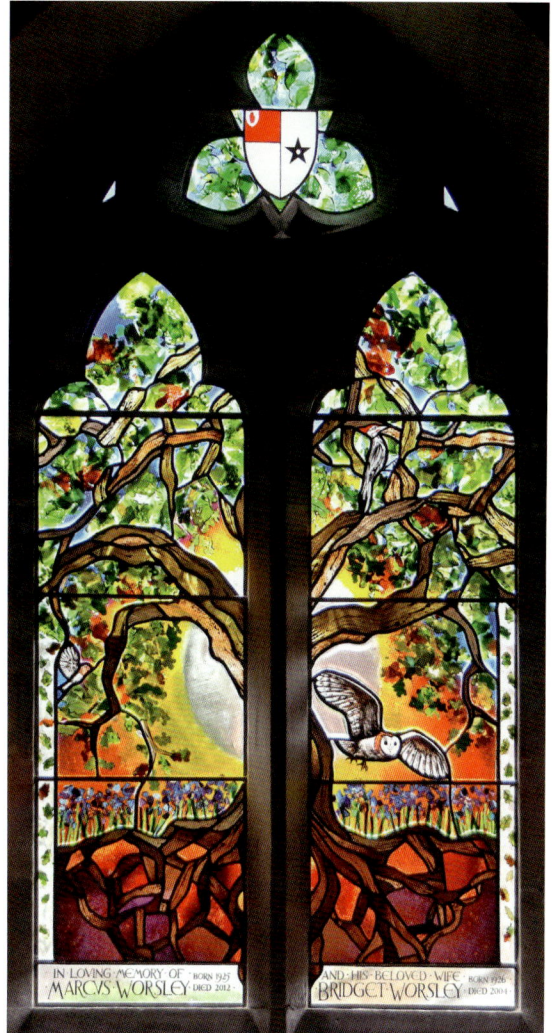

the full-scale cutlines for the glass, taking care to accurately replicate the linework.'

The collaboration demonstrates how traditional and contemporary practices can work successfully together. 'Working with Hockney gave me an opportunity to capture the spirit in his picture making and translate this into glass' (figs 4.5a–4.5b).

ALL SAINTS CHURCH, HOVINGHAM, NORTH YORKSHIRE

Helen's commission for All Saints Church, Hovingham, offered the opportunity to incorporate new techniques in glass making. 'Having attended a workshop with Narcissus Quagliata, a leading expert in the use of fused glass, I was keen to explore the possibilities of this material further. Sir William Worsley, the client at Hovingham, was open to the blending of contemporary techniques with traditional practice in his commission.'

Family histories have long been preserved through the commissioning of a window. The design for Hovingham is in memory of the donor's father, Sir Marcus Worsley, 5th Baronet and Patron of All Saints Hovingham. The Worsley family can trace their lineage to the Norman Conquest, and they have a deep connection to Hovingham, Sir Marcus Worsley having served as Chairman of the Royal Forestry Society. To reflect this, the design of the window is concerned with family, responsibility, stewardship and protection.

The fused glass elements were created with the support of Narcissus Quagliata and Judson Studios in the USA. The window incorporates an image of a sturdy oak tree, to represent rootedness, a sense of place and belonging, symbolic of a family tree, of longevity and continuity. The branches of the tree were created from leaded glass, with other areas, such as those around the owl, created from fused glass (figs 4.6a–4.6c).

4.6b   Helen Whittaker and Narcissus Quagliata, fused glass for the Worsley family memorial window, 2020, Judson Studios, California

4.6c   Detail of barn owl from the Worsley family memorial window, 2020, stained glass, All Saints Church, Hovingham

ST HELEN'S CHURCH, LEA, GAINSBOROUGH, LINCOLNSHIRE

In the commission for St Helen's Church, Lea, Gainsborough, Helen's design had to complement the 19th-century tracery lights of pressed quarry glass created by James Powell and Sons, Whitefriars. (This glass was restored by Barley Studio as part of the commission.) In the 19th century, pressed quarry glass was a contemporary development, and the thickness of the glass gives it a textural depth. The textural intensity of the Powell glass was continued by Helen, using plated, acid-etched glass to similarly create a three-dimensional effect. This window is a memorial to the Marshall family who produced steam traction engines and agricultural machinery. The design incorporates an image of a traction engine, celebrating the achievements of the Marshall company, with iconography relating to St Helen, the dedicatee of the church. In the lancets, the 'True Cross of St Helen' forms the central feature, with St Helen's, Lea, shown at the heart of the Cross. In the foreground is a Marshall traction engine, its upright chimney accentuating the shape of the Cross set against the newly ploughed earth in the background (figs 4.7a–4.7c).

far left

4.7a   Coat of arms of the Marshall family, Marshall family memorial window, 2021, detail, stained glass, St Helen's Church, Lea, Gainsborough

left

4.7b   Memorial to the Marshall family, 2021, stained glass, 150 × 320 cm, west window, north aisle, St Helen's Church, Lea, Gainsborough

right

4.7c   St Helen's Church, Marshall family memorial window, 2021, detail, stained glass, St Helen's Church, Lea, Gainsborough

SELBY ABBEY, NORTH YORKSHIRE

For Selby Abbey in North Yorkshire, a commission for a window based on the theme of the Garden of Gethsemane continued the Easter sequence established in the north nave aisle. 'I was keen to conceptualise a different image, rather than a familiar figurative representation of Christ's agony in the garden. I wanted to create a sense of entering into the darkness of the olive grove at the base of the window, then on to the central Easter focus of the crucifix and chalice, and beyond that to the lightness of the olive blossom. For me it was important for this design to speak of a progression from Christ's suffering and agony to His resurrection, using the luminous qualities of stained glass, to create a sense of transition from darkness to light by using colour and texture' (fig.4.8).

4.8 *The Agony in the Garden* (lettering by Tracey Sheppard), 2024, stained glass, 120 × 340 cm, north nave aisle, Selby Abbey

5

CONTEMPORARY CONTEXTS

Helen's work can be found in hospitals, schools, community centres, exhibition halls, hotels, offices and private houses, as well as in sacred buildings. Wherever the location, Helen's windows are commissioned to decorate a space, tell a story or celebrate and/or commemorate an event. The artistic language Helen uses is broad-ranging, from figurative work through to abstract or symbolic designs. Developments in lighting technology have also provided opportunities for windows to be shown in dark or windowless space as panels can easily be lit evenly and viewed as she intended. The use of back-lit stained-glass panels or 'paintings in glass' for interior spaces, such as in galleries, brings new opportunities for Helen to use more experimental techniques. The possibility to view the work close-up provides a captivating and immersive experience for the viewer.

Working to commission is something that defines Helen's identity as an artist. Each project begins with an open mind, to its possibilities in style and technique, whether the final work is figurative, abstract or symbolic. This section presents the breadth of Helen's contemporary responses to a range of contexts: sacred, secular and domestic.

ST JOSEPH'S ROMAN CATHOLIC CHURCH, OAKHAM, RUTLAND

The brief for Helen's new glazing scheme for St Joseph's Roman Catholic Church, Oakham, was to ensure that the interior of this 1970s' building

5.1a   Lily glazing scheme, 2017–18, stained glass, 27 sq m, St Joseph's Roman Catholic Church, Oakham

5.1b   Helen Whittaker painting the lily glazing scheme, 2017–18, stained glass, 27 sq m, Barley Studio, Dunnington, York

remained light and bright whilst also obscuring the exterior view. The theme of lilies was chosen to reference St Joseph – the lily is his emblem – and the Virgin Mary – lilies are associated with her innocence and purity. The flowers in this scheme are drawn as larger-than-life, with each window showing a slightly different perspective of the flower against a background of dark and light blue, with occasional flashes of green from the stems and leaves. The multiple views work to provide an abstract pattern across the entire scheme. The slight changes in the panorama help to bring a sense of gentle movement to the interior. Helen's choice of exuberant, naturalistic lilies complements the dark and austere interior of the church. Helen's work replaced clear glazing and demonstrates how stained glass can be used to meet changing needs and a congregation's expectations in terms of both content and style (figs 5.1a and 5.1b).

OUR LADY OF LOURDES CATHOLIC CHAPEL, FILINVEST CITY, ALABANG, PHILIPPINES

In 2019, Helen was commissioned to design a scheme of six large windows for a planned new building in the Philippines. Our Lady of Lourdes Catholic Chapel, Filinvest City, Alabang was designed by Japanese architect Hiroshi Nakamura. The unusually shaped windows are set within the sweeping curves of the structure and resemble a large lily flower. 'The repeating geometrical patterns in each of the six windows are designed to suggest a rosary of lilies. The central section of each window contains symbols referring to the Virgin Mary and her associated apparitions.' Helen's rich design combines colour, geometry, pattern and symbolism to create an atmosphere of contemplation within the chapel. 'Each window uses a single colour range so that when seen in situ the windows evoke a rainbow within the building' (figs 5.2a–5.2c).

5.2a   Exterior of Our Lady of Lourdes Catholic Chapel, Alabang

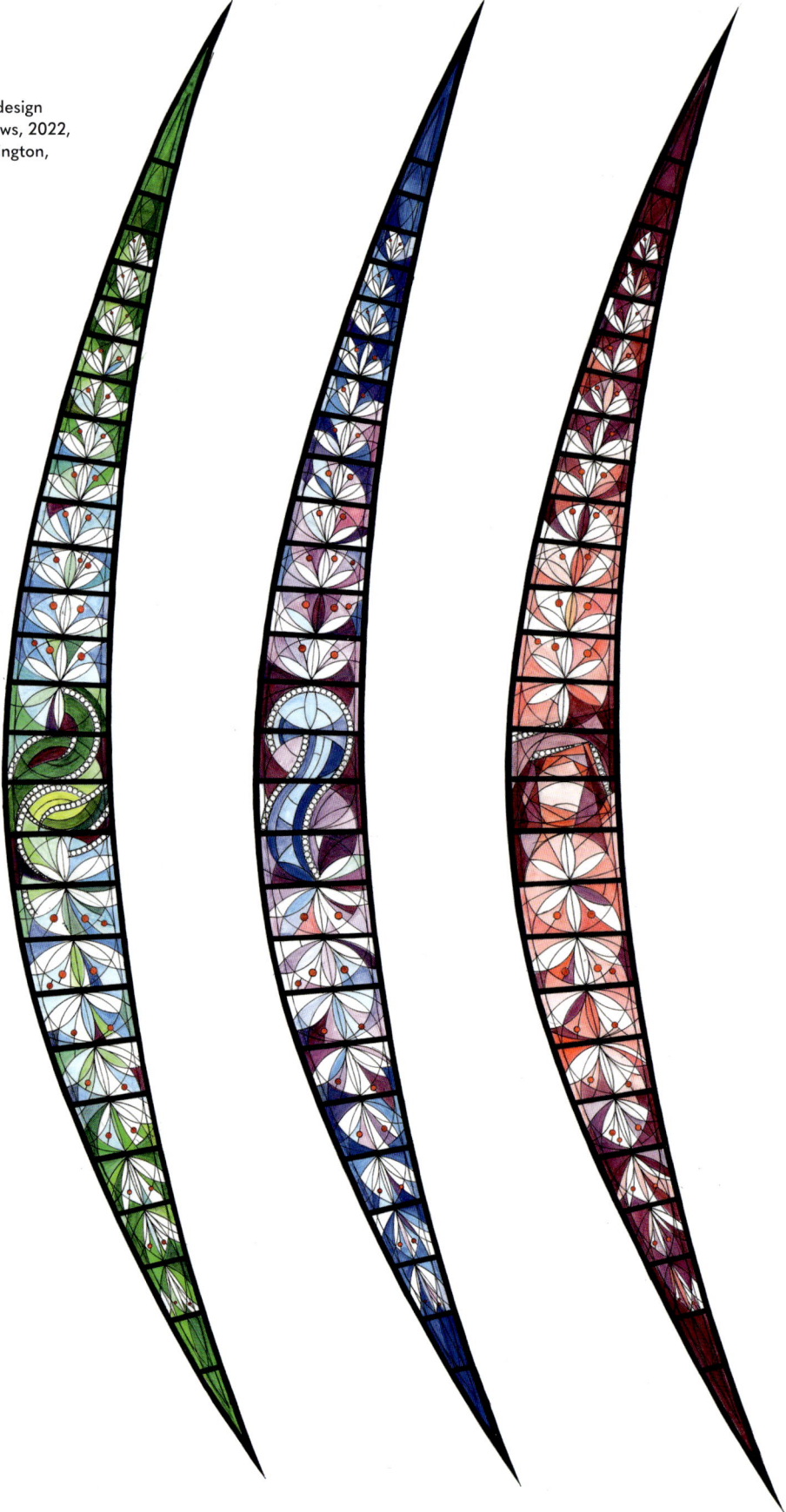

5.2b   Watercolour design
for six Marian windows, 2022,
Barley Studio, Dunnington,
York

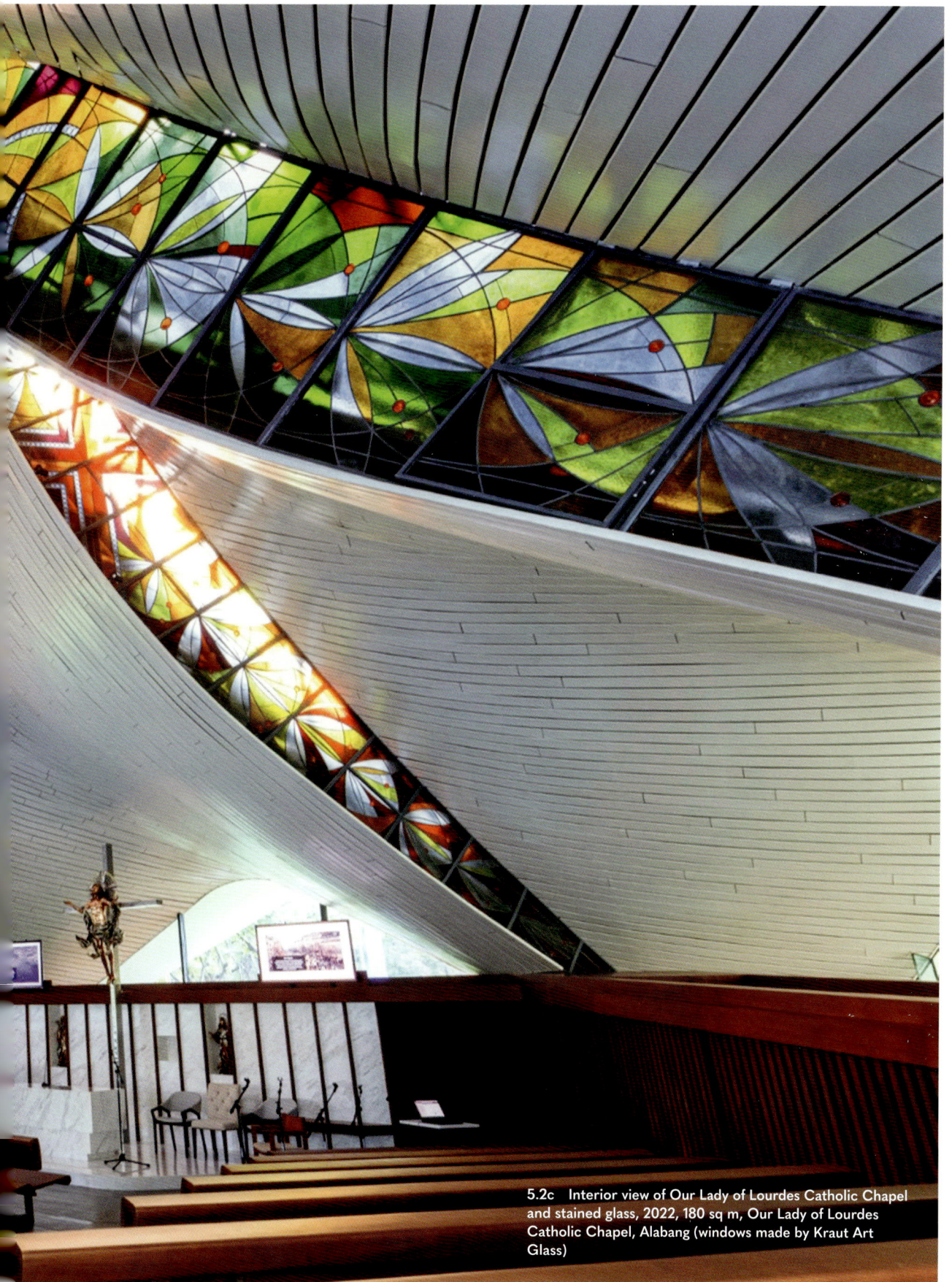

5.2c   Interior view of Our Lady of Lourdes Catholic Chapel and stained glass, 2022, 180 sq m, Our Lady of Lourdes Catholic Chapel, Alabang (windows made by Kraut Art Glass)

5.3 The *Hope* window, 2024, stained glass, 140 × 400 cm, St Michael's Church, Highgate, London

ST MICHAEL'S CHURCH, HIGHGATE, LONDON

The initial concept for the *Hope* window for St Michael's Church, Highgate, London (fig.5.3), began as a figurative design to sit alongside the other figurative works in the church, including Evie Hone's east window, the *Last Supper*.[1] After consultation with the client, it was agreed that a non-figurative, geometric design would work well. 'I wanted to create a window which emulates but does not compete with the boldness of Hone's figurative work.' Helen was inspired by Evie Hone's contemporary responses to traditional sacred themes, and by other pioneering female artists of the time. Sonia Delaunay's abstract and colourful geometric patterns provided particular inspiration for Helen's response to the commission. The *Hope* window explores the idea of the Trinity through vibrant colour, with the 'cross of Faith' and the 'anchor of Hope' being connected through concentric circles. 'I wanted to create a joyful and uplifting experience for all who will see the window.'

ST MARY'S CHURCH, SOPWORTH, WILTSHIRE

The *Creation* window for St Mary's Church, Sopworth, was originally exhibited at the *Prince and Patron* exhibition (2018) at Buckingham Palace in honour of King Charles' 70th birthday and to highlight the monarch's role in commissioning and supporting a diverse range of art, artists and cultures. The *Creation* window is a memorial to a young man who spent his final months engaged in community service in Kenya and Tanzania. 'For this design I made particular reference to the wildlife of East Africa and the tropical coast.' The design comprises seven concentric circles, each one representing a day as described in the story of the Creation in the book of Genesis. 'The circles remind us of the western medieval understanding of God's role as the divine geometer and as architect of the universe' (fig.5.4).

5.4 *Creation*, memorial window for Ned Sells (lettering by Phil Thomas), 2018, stained glass, 40 × 100 cm, north nave aisle, St Mary's Church, Sopworth

HAW PAR MANSION, HONG KONG

Helen was commissioned to create the exhibition panel *Time and Space* as part of her involvement in the 'GREAT Britain' UK government campaign to showcase British talent in the creative sector. *Time and Space* celebrates the reopening of Haw Par Mansion, Hong Kong, as a music education centre. The Mansion was built in 1935 and was originally the home of Aw Boon Haw, entrepreneur, philanthropist and founder of the Tiger Balm ointment company. The Mansion's Moon Gate is the focal point of its front elevation and so Helen chose this architectural feature as the centre of her design and her inspiration for the entire panel. 'The full moon signifies the start of a new phase in the lunar calendar so it perfectly suited the celebratory intention of the commission, with Haw Par Mansion entering a new phase of its history.' The Moon Gate is set within a representation of the

solar system and the colours of the planets speak to the five elements of traditional Chinese medicine, as well as referencing the 'music of the spheres', in keeping with the Mansion's use as a centre for music education (fig.5.5).

ART MACAU, MACAU, CHINA

Following the exhibition at the Haw Par Mansion in Hong Kong, Helen was invited to exhibit a panel in the London Pavilion of Art Macau, the 2023 Macau International Art Biennale. Inspired by the theme 'Cathedrals of the Twenty-first Century', Helen chose to juxtapose the traditional Christian religion of the West with the ancient Chinese belief system of Confucianism in her panel *God Does Not Play Dice with the Universe* (fig.5.6). Both offer a framework to live by, valuing personal ethics and morality within a wider society. 'In thinking about

5.5 *Time and Space*, exhibition panel, 2019, stained glass, 50 × 40 cm, Haw Par Mansion, Hong Kong

5.6   *God Does Not Play Dice with the Universe*, exhibition panel, 2023,
stained glass, 25× 40 cm, Art Macau, Macau

the similarities and differences between these ideas, I feel I am following in the footsteps of the 16th-century Italian priest Matteo Ricci, who came to Macao during the Jesuit China Missions. Ricci created a bridge between Western and Eastern thought, translating Euclid into Chinese and Confucius into Latin.'

Across the world, people are moving away from traditional religion towards new beliefs. In Macau, this shift is exemplified by the huge gaming industry, with its ideas of luck, chance and destiny. 'I bring these contrasting ideologies together with the cross shape of a die box template overlaid on to the cruciform floor plan of St Paul's Cathedral. A roulette wheel spins over the central crossing of the Cathedral, its circular shape symbolising the notion of eternity in Christianity and harmony – the balance of the yin and yang – in Chinese philosophy. Around the circle, the skyline of London contrasts the modern 21st-century city with the historic St Paul's Cathedral at its centre.'

MERCHANT TAYLORS' HALL, YORK

While stained glass has long been associated with ecclesiastical buildings, the interiors of secular buildings, both public and private, can also be transformed with its light and colour.

In 2014, a dendrochronological investigation of the roof timbers of the Great Hall of the Company of Merchant Taylors in York established its build date as 1415. This discovery prompted the Company to commission Helen to create a design incorporating the Company's coat of arms into the plain glazing of the three windows in the east end of the Great Hall. 'My design creates a strong impact as you enter the room. The coat of arms is the focal point, shown as if sewn onto silk. The surrounding fabric flows across the remaining glazing and into the flanking windows.' The anniversary dates are shown embroidered in gold thread below the coat of arms, with a large, threaded, silver needle just below, adding the finishing touches to the stitching.

The design and techniques used follow in the footsteps of a window created by the noted York stained glass artist Henry Gyles in 1662, and now in the Little Hall. Helen's window adopts the same glazing pattern of rectangular squares, and uses no coloured glass – only yellow stain, glass paints and coloured enamels.

Heraldry often appears in English stained glass dating as far back as the 12th century. Through the abstracted silk design and the sculptural element of the needle 'sewn' into the glass, Helen has ensured that the coat of arms references the long history of the Merchant Taylors and their continuing presence in the City of York (figs 5.7a and 5.7b).

5.7a *Celebrating 600 Years of the Hall*, 2016, stained glass, 650 × 290 cm, Merchant Taylors' Hall, York

5.7b *Celebrating 600 Years of the Hall*, 2016, detail, needle and thread, copper, brass and stained glass, Merchant Taylors' Hall, York

DULWICH COLLEGE, LONDON

Helen's design for Dulwich College was commissioned to mark 400 years of the school's foundation. Set in the Lower Hall, often referred to as the heart of the College, the window incorporates the flaming heart from the coat of arms of the College set against a patterned and entwining network of spirals, referencing the wrought-iron main gates of the College. Helen's fretwork design seeks to connect the viewer to the school and its distinguished history, as well as to its immediate built environment (fig.5.8).

PRIVATE COMMISSIONS

Private commissions are often led by the client's vision. For a private home in York, the clients requested stained-glass panels for their front door and transom above. 'Aware of the clients' fondness for work by John Piper, John Brunsdon and Donald Hamilton Fraser, and their collection of modern art, along with a passion for sailing, I wanted to create a design which complemented their interests and artworks. Using a palette of white, blue, orange and teal I created a design from fragmented pieces which, when viewed from a distance, took the form of sails, hull and keel of a boat and waves of the sea' (fig.5.9).

For a home in Whitby, North Yorkshire, the client requested an abstract window design in textured glass using soft colours which would transmit a sense of the surrounding scenery (fig.5.10). The leaded windows were commissioned by an enthusiastic photographer with an interest in science and art. 'Using a simple palette of clear textured and opalescent glasses I was able to capture the play of light and movement of falling water. As the lighting alters throughout the day, the appearance changes with the textures of the glass, sometimes absorbing and at other times projecting the natural colours from the garden in ever-changing patterns.'

5.8 *Celebrating 400 Years of the School*, 2019, stained glass,
200 × 70 cm, Lower Hall, Dulwich College, London

CONCLUSION

Stained-glass windows have a long and rich tradition as a narrative form and as an aesthetic and spiritual medium. The light transmitted through windows is often described as ethereal or uplifting, which perhaps explains why stained glass has retained its popularity over the centuries, as audiences relate to the cascades of coloured light within a space and the emotions those colours can inspire. Today, the range of techniques open to a designer expands the possibility of a window as a medium for engagement and reflection in secular as well as religious contexts.

Keith Barley's central ethos has always been to honour the artist's intention, both in conserving historic windows and translating new design ideas into glass. Helen Whittaker's artworks highlight the power of stained glass to engage the viewer in a range of contexts and settings. Close collaboration between artists, conservators and craftspeople is a key part of Barley Studio's practice, working alongside expert advisors to ensure that the highest standards are maintained.

In 2023, the Studio celebrated '50 years of Design and Mastery in Stained Glass', having preserved some of the finest stained glass in the country and created new work to continue this legacy. We continue to shine a light on this unique art form and its potential to enhance our surroundings and those of future generations. Such passion and expertise are essential in ensuring that the rich heritage and skills of stained glass are maintained and continue to be cared for and celebrated.

NOTES

INTRODUCTION

1 https://heritagecrafts.org.uk/redlist/.
2 John Piper, *Stained Glass: art or anti-art*, Studio Vista, London, 1968, p.10.

1 CONSERVATION AND RESTORATION

1 Dr Peter Anthony Newton FSA (1935–1987) was an iconographer and historian of medieval stained glass. He read History of Art at the Courtauld Institute and went on to gain his PhD at the University of London. Newton became Mellon Lecturer in British Medieval Art at the University of York in 1965, where he was also instrumental in setting up the Department of Medieval Studies, and served York Minster as academic adviser to the York Glaziers' Trust.
2 'Quarries' are small panes of glass, usually diamonds, squares or rectangles, leaded into a repeating geometric pattern. From Latin, *quadrus* (square).
3 Architectural Society of the Archdeaconry of Northampton, *Architectural Notices of the Churches of the Archdeaconry of Northampton: Deaneries of Higham Ferrers and Haddon*, John Henry Parker, London, 1849, p. 228.
4 Pers. comm., Philip Lankester, 1983.
5 Corpus Vitrearum, *Guidelines for the Conservation and Restoration of Stained Glass*, 2nd edn, Nuremberg, 2004.
6 Margaret Aston, *England's Iconoclasts Volume I: Laws Against Images,* Clarendon Press, Oxford, 1988, p.256.

7 Keith Barley, 'Conservation and Restoration', in Sarah Brown and Lindsay MacDonald, eds, *Fairford Parish Church*, Sutton Publishing Ltd, Stroud, 2007, p.113.
8 *Saint Matthias*, panel, *c.*1500–1515, https://collections.vam.ac.uk/item/O97663/saint-matthias-panel-unknown/. Accessed 22 February 2024.
9 Sarah Brown and Lindsay MacDonald, eds, *Fairford Parish Church*, Sutton Publishing Ltd, Stroud, 2007, p.114, pp 118–19.
10 Harold William Harvey (22 November 1922 – 29 January 2011), usually known as Harry, was a leading figure in contemporary stained glass design and completed more than 220 windows in a prolific career lasting 40 years. He moved to York in 1947 as assistant to Harry Stammers, who had been invited by Dean Milner-White to revive the York School of Glass Painting. Notable works include the East window of York's Guildhall (1960), St Wilfrid in Ripon Cathedral (1977) and the decoration of the Astronomical Clock in York Minster.
11 Pers. comm., John Malleson, Chair of Friends of Fairford Church, 16 April 1991.
12 Pers. comm., Jill Kerr (English Heritage) to Mr Malleson, Fairford, 12 June 1991.
13 Keith C. Barley, '"Man in a Red Hat": St Mary's Church, Fairford: The Creation of a Remarkable Late Medieval Glazing Scheme', Master's thesis, University of York, 2015, https://etheses.whiterose.ac.uk/14278/1/KC%20Barley%20MA%20Vol1%20final.pdf.

14 Nicholas Patrick Reyntiens OBE (11 December 1925 – 25 October 2021), usually known as Patrick, was a British stained-glass artist who collaborated with John Piper for over 35 years. Their notable works together include the Baptistry window of Coventry Cathedral (1957–61) and the lantern windows of Liverpool Metropolitan Cathedral (1962–67). Solo works include windows for St Michael and All Angels, Marden (1962), St Martin's Church, Sandford (1974).

15 Pers. comm., Sarah Brown, 2013.

2 CREATIVITY AND CRAFT

1 Keith Barry Critchlow (16 March 1933 – 8 April 2020) was a British artist, architect, lecturer, author and sacred geometer. He was Professor of Islamic Art at the Royal College of Art in London from 1975, where he founded the Visual Islamic and Traditional Arts (VITA) department in 1984. Critchlow was an acknowledged expert on Chartres Cathedral, and co-founder and President of the Temenos Academy in the UK. Notable publications include *Order in Space: A Design Source Book* (1969) and *The Hidden Geometry of Flowers: Living Rhythms Form and Number* (2011).

2 Harold Gosney (b. 16 September 1937) is an artist and sculptor. Born in Sheffield, he studied at the Grimsby School of Art and the Slade School of Fine Art in London. He returned to teach at the Grimsby School of Art in 1960 and moved to York on his retirement in 1992 to continue his career as a sculptor. Gosney's work is on display in the cathedrals of York, Ripon and Chester, and he has made a significant contribution to public art in Grimsby.

3 Luke 8:4–5 (English Standard Version).

4 Walt Whitman, 'The Untold Want', *Leaves of Grass* (1881).

3 CONCEPT TO CREATION

1 The term 'Verre Églomisé' derives from Jean-Baptise Glomy, an 18th-century antiques dealer based in Paris, who enhanced his prints and embroideries with glass matts painted black, and strips of gold paper for borders. See Rudy Eswarin, 'Terminology of *Verre Églomisé*', *Journal of Glass Studies*, vol.21, 1979, pp 98–101.

5 CONTEMPORARY CONTEXTS

1 Eva Sydney Hone RHA (22 April 1894 – 13 March 1955), usually known as Evie, was an Irish painter and stained-glass artist. She is considered to be an early pioneer of cubism, although her best-known works are stained glass. Her most notable pieces are the east window in the chapel at Eton College, which depicts the Crucifixion, and *My Four Green Fields*, which is now in the Government Buildings in Dublin.

BIBLIOGRAPHY

Architectural Society of the Archdeaconry of Northampton, *Architectural Notices of the Churches of the Archdeaconry of Northampton: Deaneries of Higham Ferrers and Haddon*, J.H. Parker, London, 1849

Aston, Margaret, *England's Iconoclasts, Volume I: Laws against Images,* Clarendon Press, Oxford, 1988

Barley, Keith, 'Conservation and Restoration', in Sarah Brown and Lindsay MacDonald, eds, *Fairford Parish Church*, Sutton Publishing Ltd, Stroud, 2007

The Bible (English Standard Version)

Brown, Sarah, and Lindsay MacDonald, eds, *Fairford Parish Church*, Sutton Publishing Ltd, Stroud, 2007

Corpus Vitrearum, *Guidelines for the Conservation and Restoration of Stained Glass*, 2nd edn, Nuremberg, 2004, available at: www.cvma.ac.uk/conserv/index.html

McBrinn, Joseph, 'Evie Hone (1894–1955)', in Nicola Gordon Bowe, David Caron and Michael Wynne, eds, *Gazetteer of Irish Stained Glass: The Works of Harry Clarke, the Artists of An Túr Gloine (The Tower of Glass) and Artists of Succeeding Generations to the Present Day*, Irish Academic Press, Newbridge, Co. Kildare, 2021 (Revised Edition), pp 264–6

Piper, J., *Stained Glass: art or anti-art*, Studio Vista, London, 1968

INDEX

Note: *italic* page numbers indicate figures; page numbers followed by n. refer to notes

Abergavenny (Monmouthshire), St Mary's Priory Church, 'Jesse' window (Whittaker, 2016) *60*, 61, *61*

Ashton Under Lyne (Greater Manchester), St Michael and All Angels' Church 12

back-lit stained glass 73
Banks, Tony 45, 62
Barley, Keith 7, 9–17, 90
Barley Studio 7, 9, 12, 14, *15*, 19, 37, *41*, *53*, 57, 65, *74*, 90
Becket reliquary 31
Beilby, Nick 55
Beverley Minster (East Yorkshire) *Pilgrimage* (Whittaker, 2004) 21–2, 22, 23, *24–5*, 26, *27*
Brancepeth (Durham), St Brandon's, *Paradise Window* (Whittaker, 2014) *30*, 31
Brown, Sarah 15

cartoons 37, *53*, 65
Catherine of Siena 44, 45
CCC (Council for the Care of Churches) 10
Chartres Cathedral (France) 19, 49, 92 n.1
China, Art Macau Biennale, *God Does Not Play Dice with the Universe* exhibition panel (Whittaker, 2023) 82–4, *83*
conservation/restoration 7, 8, 9–18, 57
    19th century hostility towards 9–10, 11

collaboration in 14, 15
craft/art in 14–15
and environmental protection 9, 12
and European techniques 12
Corpus Vitrearum (CVMA) 9, 12
Council for the Care of Churches (CCC) 10
Crayke (North Yorkshire), St Cuthbert's Church, *St Cuthbert* (Whittaker, 2020) 53–4, *53*, *54*
Critchlow, Keith Barry 19, 92 n.1

Defoe, Daniel 14
Delaunay, Sonia 81
design of stained glass
    art/craft in 14–15
    and history/architectural style of building 37, 49
    and individual response to commissions 7, 19, 37
    lettering in 21, 28
    and mixed media/sculpture 21, 22, 44, 49, 53
    and narrative 15, 37
    and viewing perspectives 45, 59, 75

Elizabeth II *64*, 65–7, *65*, *66*
Ellerton (East Yorkshire), St Mary and St Lawrence's Church, east window (Whittaker, 2003) 58–9, *58*, *59*
Ely Cathedral (Cambridgeshire) 9
    New Processional Way (Whittaker, 2000) *36*, 37–9, *38–9*
English Heritage 12, 14

Fairford (Gloucestershire), St Mary's Church 7, 12–15
    and 19th century replacement of Great West Window 14
    east window 12, *13*, 14
fused glass 67, *68–9*

Gilbert, Michael 45, 62
Gosney, Harold 22, 92 n.2
Greatford (Lincolnshire), St Thomas of Canterbury Church, *Becket Window* (Whittaker, 2015) 31–3, *31*

Hakluyt, Richard 33
Hart (County Durham), St Mary Magdalene, *Parable of the Sower* (Whittaker, 2018) *32*, 33
Harvey, Harold William 14, 91 n.10
Hockney, David 65–7, *65*, *66*
Hone, Evie 81, 92 n.1
Hong Kong, Haw Par Mansion, *Time and Space* exhibition panel (Whittaker, 2019) *82*, *82*
Hovingham (North Yorkshire), All Saints Church, Worsley family memorial window (Whittaker, 2020) 67–9, *67*, *68–9*

Judson Studios (USA) 67

Kempe, Charles Eamer 39
Kirknewton (Northumberland), St Gregory's Church, Josephine Butler memorial (Whittaker, 2006) 44, *44*

Lea, Gainsborough (Lincolnshire), St Helen's Church, Marshall family memorial window (Whittaker, 2021) 70–71, *70, 71*

Lindisfarne Gospels 53

Lockington (East Yorkshire), St Mary's Church, *Parable of the Sower* (Whittaker, 2010) 28–9, *28, 29*

London
Dulwich College, *Celebrating 400 Years of the School* (Whittaker, 2019) 86, *87*
Prince and Patron exhibition (Buckingham Palace, 2018) 81
Royal Air Force Club, Piccadilly, *Celebrating Women in the RAF* window (Whittaker, 2018) 62–4, *62, 63, 64*
Royal Air Force Club, Piccadilly, staircase window (Whittaker, 2008) 45–7, *45, 46, 47*
St Ethelburga's Centre for Reconciliation and Peace, *St Ethelburga* (Whittaker, 2002) 39–40, *40*
St Michael's, Highgate, *Hope* window (Whittaker, 2024) 80–81, *80*
Westminster Abbey, *Queen's Window* (Hockney, 2018) 65–7, *65, 66*

Marks, Richard 11–12, 14

Nakamura, Hiroshi 75
Newton, Peter 9, 11, 91 n.1

Oakham (Rutland), St Joseph's Roman Catholic Church, lily glazing scheme (Whittaker, 2017–18) 73–5, *73, 74*
Ortelius, Abraham 33

Philippines, Our Lady of Lourdes Catholic Church, Alabang, Marian windows (Whittaker, 2022) 75–9, *75, 76–7, 78–9*
Piper, John 7, 92 n.14

private commissions 86, *88, 89*
protective glazing systems 12

Quagliata, Narcissus 67, *68–9*
quarries 9, 33, 91 n.2

restoration *see* conservation/ restoration
Reyntiens, Nicholas Patrick 15, *15*, 92 n.14
Ricci, Matteo 84

Scarborough Hospital Chapel (East Yorkshire), *Prayer Tree* (Whittaker, 2019) 52–3, *52*
Selby Abbey (North Yorkshire), *Agony in the Garden* (Whittaker, 2024) *72, 72*
Sheffield (South Yorkshire), St Mary's Church, Community and Conference Centre, *Pilgrimage* (Whittaker, 2008) 48–50, *48, 49, 50*
Sheppard, Tracey 33, *34–5, 72*
Smith, Charles *28, 43*
Sopworth (Wiltshire), St Mary's Church, *Creation* window (Whittaker, 2018) 81, *81*
Southwell Minster (Nottinghamshire) 15–17, *16, 17*
Stancliffe, Martin 15
Stanford on Avon (Northamptonshire), St Nicholas' Church 7, 9–12, *11,* 14, 15
Eagle of St John tracery panel 10–11, *10*
Stevens Architectural Glass Competition 19, 59
Stowmarket (Suffolk), St Peter and St Mary's Church, *The Four Seasons* (Whittaker, 2005-6) 41–3, *41, 42*

Thomas, Phil *32, 55, 56, 67, 81*
Tree of Jesse (Whittaker, 1998) 57–9, *57*

Verre Églomisé 45, 92 n.1

Warndon (Worcestershire), St Nicholas' Church *8,* 9

Wetheringsett (Suffolk), All Saints Church, *Axis Mundi* (Whittaker, 2023) 33–5, *43–5*
Whitby (North Yorkshire), *Falling Water* (Whittaker, private commission, 2017) 86, *89*
Whitman, Walt 33, 92 n.4
Whittaker, Helen
background/training of 19
and Barley 14
and experimental techniques 73
and Hockney 65–7
and individual response to commissions 7, 19, 37
and medieval glass 57–9
and mixed media/sculpture 21, 22, 44, 49, 53
narrative in designs of 15, 37
and old/new approaches combined 57
and private commissions 86, *88, 89*
and Quagliata 67, *68–9*
and viewing perspectives 45, 59, 75
see also towns/cities featuring specific works
Winston, Charles 9–10, *10,* 11
Worksop Priory (Nottinghamshire), *St Cuthbert* (Whittaker, 2003) *18,* 20, 21, *21*

York (North Yorkshire)
All Saints Church, Afghanistan window (Whittaker, 2015) 50–51, *50, 51*
Boats (private commission, Whittaker, 2015) 86, *88*
Merchant Taylor's Hall, *Celebrating 600 Years of the Hall* (Whittaker, 2016) 84–6, *84–5, 86*
St Lawrence's Church, D-Day Landings window (Whittaker, 2020) 55–6, *55, 56*
York Glaziers Trust 9, 15, 91 n.1
York Minster 9, 12, 91 nn 1 and 10, 92 n.2

ACKNOWLEDGEMENTS

Over the past 50 years, Barley Studio has strived for excellence in design and mastery of stained glass. Directors Keith Barley and Helen Whittaker thank all those who have worked with Barley Studio over the years, from team members to clients and supporters. By shining a light on our exploration of creativity, conservation and craft, we hope the beauty of stained glass is illuminated for future generations to enjoy.

The authors would particularly like to thank the Barley Studio team, especially Alison Gilchrist for her assistance in putting this book together. For Keith's work at Fairford: John Malleson, Denis Hodgson OBE and Jill Kerr. For their support and guidance during Helen's career: Harold Gosney, Harry Howard, David and Jenny Olive, Phil Thomas, Toklis Tombros and Marylyn Whittaker. For their support of this publication: Edinburgh University and Edinburgh College of Art. For his long-standing support of heritage and craft skills, HM King Charles III.

* * *

Except where noted, all quotations are from conversations with Helen Whittaker and Keith Barley.